UTAH BEACH

TUESDAY 6TH JUNE 1944

GIs taking shelter behind the antitank wall on the edge of the beach, whilst others advance across the dunes amidst the fog of war. © NARA

Christophe PRIME

UTAH BEACH
TUESDAY 6TH JUNE 1944

OREP
EDITIONS

CONTENTS

INTRODUCTION .... P. 6

PART 1 : CODENAME 'UTAH' .... P. 9

PART 2 : THE NIGHT THE PARAS JUMPED .... P. 51

PART 3 : THE AMPHIBIOUS ASSAULT .... P. 83

PART 4 : THE UTAH BRIDGEHEAD AFTER THE 6TH OF JUNE .... P. 107

BIBLIOGRAPHY .... P. 128

ACKNOWLEDGEMENTS .... P. 128

This picture shows what Gooseberry G1 looked like a few months after the end of unloading operations. © Rights reserved

These men from the 1st ESB have dug out their foxholes alongside the antitank wall near Utah Beach. This picture was taken at high tide on the 7th of June. The weather was dull, as illustrated by the flag, the heavy skies and the seamen's warm clothing.
© NARA

INTRODUCTION

Decided on early 1944 to enable the American troops to take control of the port of Cherbourg as quickly as possible, the landings on Utah Beach were both the most complex and the most risky combined operations the Allies had to undertake on the 6th of June. The isolated future bridgehead, the configuration of the terrain and the presence of massive German forces in the area had obliged the Allied command to plan a nocturnal airborne assault to secure vital intersections, such as Sainte-Mère-Église, and to pave the way for the landed Allied troops to advance.

Not as intensely dramatic as the events on Omaha Beach, the attention afforded to the battle that was waged on Utah in the collective memory is of a more

'We'll start the war from right here!'
Brigadier General Teddy Roosevelt Jr. (1887-1944)

discreet nature. Yet its story, far more complex than one would imagine, is a fascinating one.

This book aims at offering you an insight into the whys and wherefores of this extraordinary operation and a delve into the terrible battle waged by the paras from the 101st and the 82nd US Airborne Divisions, alongside the 4th US Infantry Division. For a whole week, American and German soldiers waged a fragmented battle of rare intensity in the heart of the marshes and Normandy's typical bocage landscape. You will also learn of Utah's Gooseberry which, along with a similar installation on Omaha, contributed considerably to the American war effort in Normandy.

The sound of the guns gradually moved away from the beach. American soldiers landed at low tide and gathered together on the beach. The sandbanks obliged the Landing Craft Vehicle Personnel to ground around 100 metres from the shoreline.
© NARA

PART 1

CODENAME 'UTAH'

EARLY PLANS

As soon as they engaged together in the conflict, the United States and Great Britain needed to define a common military strategy. They initially agreed to concentrate their efforts on countering Germany.

The US Army staff, commanded by Major General George C. Marshall, was in favour of a landing operation on the northwest coast of Europe, 'as soon as possible', convinced that only a powerful frontal attack could enable them to overthrow the loathed enemy. As from January 1942, the War Plans Division began to draft the provisional invasion plan; however, with memories of the bloody battles in Somme and Passchendeale still fresh in their memories, Churchill and the rest of the British high command were more reluctant, preferring to attack the enemy on a second front. Roosevelt did his best to convince Churchill of their strategy's worth.

On the 8th of April 1942, Marshall and the US President's diplomatic advisor, Harry Hopkins, travelled to Great Britain to plead in favour of two projects to land on the Western European coast. A large-scale operation, codenamed Round Up was to be organised in the spring of 1943, between the ports of Le Havre and Boulogne-sur-Mer. The initial plan involved a total of 48 divisions, 30 of which would be American, together with 5,800 planes and no less than 7,000 ships. However, they all knew that it would take long months before the war machine was entirely operational and the necessary equipment manufactured in requisitioned factories.

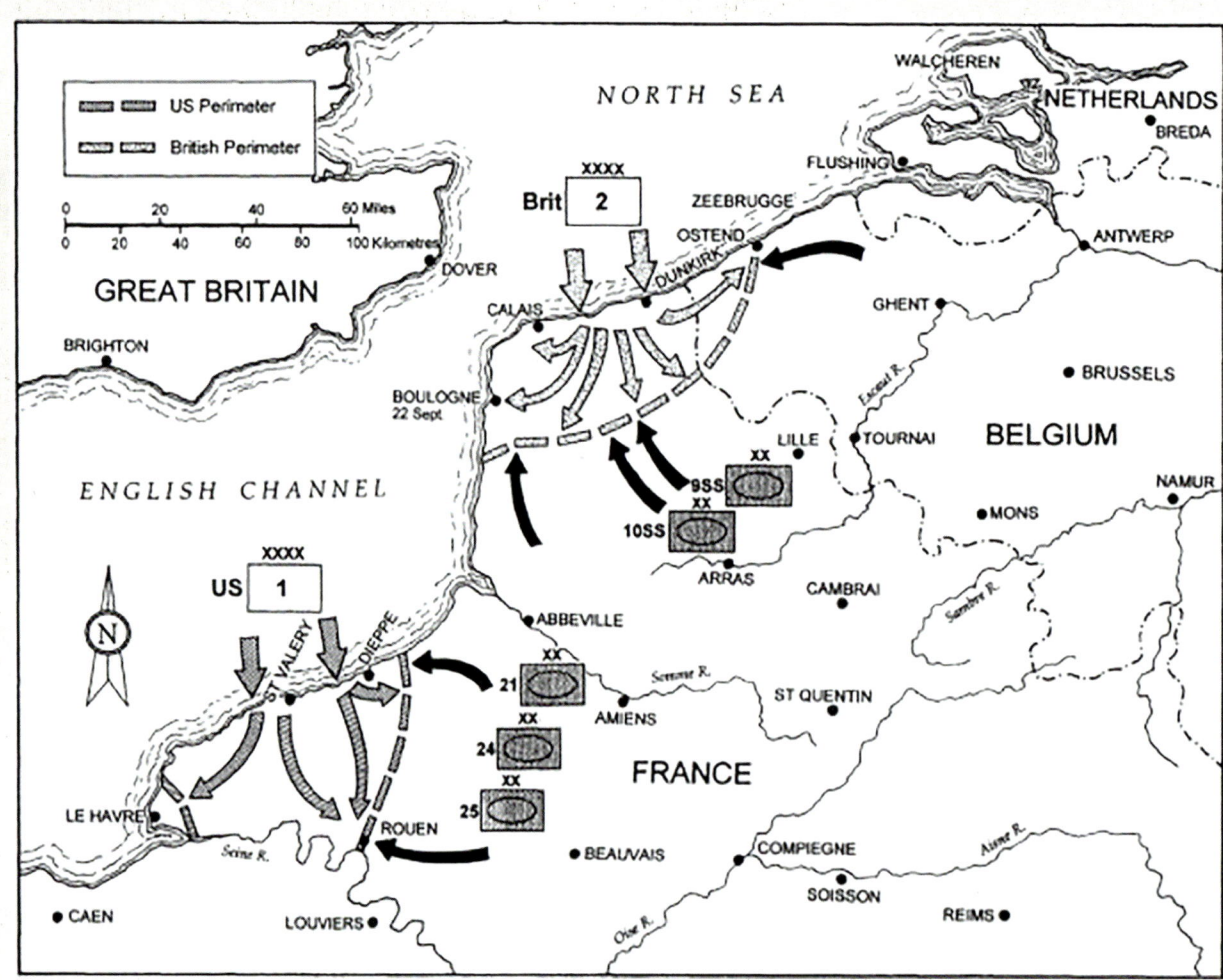

Plans for operation Sledgehammer. © Rights reserved

American contingents were sent to Britain in increasingly large numbers. © NARA

Soldiers from an anti-aircraft instruction unit on an assault course at Camp Edwards (Massachusetts). © NARA

'I am becoming more and more interested in the establishment of this new front this summer, certainly for air and raids. From the point of view of shipping and supplies it is infinitely easier for us to participate in because of a maximum distance of about three thousand miles. And even though losses will doubtless be great, such losses will be compensated by at least equal German losses and by compelling Germans to divert large forces of all kinds from Russian fronts.'

Letter from Roosevelt to Churchill, dated 9th March 1942.

Another combined operation on a lesser scale, codenamed Sledgehammer, was therefore scheduled to be launched in the Cotentin peninsula during the month of September 1942. The aim was to take control of the port of Cherbourg in order to stall Stalin who was desperately urging for the opening of a second front. The plan was for the US Army to bear the brunt of the effort. This continental bridgehead would need to be secured the entire winter, pending the launch of operation Round Up.

Although feasible on paper, Sledgehammer could but end in a fiasco. At this point in time, the Allies lacked the necessary resources to lead such an operation. Furthermore, the *Wehrmacht* had posted a total of thirty divisions in the West. The failed Anglo–Canadian operation in Dieppe on the 19th of August 1942 was to prove the impracticability of such an enterprise at this stage in the conflict.

As illustrated by this poster, nothing was to stop the American war machine. © NARA

Marshall and the War Secretary Henry L. Stimson, during talks on the war in Europe at the War Department in January 1942. © NARA

A COMMON STRATEGY

Whilst the Red Army continued to lead the war effort in the East, the Anglo-American armies had landed in North Africa to chase out the German and Italian forces, before launching a direct attack on fascist Italy, which was considered as the soft underbelly of the Axis powers. It was in Anfa, on the outskirts of Casablanca, that Roosevelt and Churchill finally agreed on the strategy to adopt, and began to plan the liberation of Western Europe. The date scheduled for the landings on the Western European coast was set for the spring of 1944.

A joint inter-allied staff was set up to plan operations. On the 12th of March, Lieutenant General Frederick E. Morgan was appointed Chief of Staff to Supreme Allied Commander (COSSAC). He was assisted by US Army Brigadier

Roosevelt and Churchill during the last press conference in the villa gardens at Casablanca. It was on this occasion that the American President informally announced that they would accept no less than unconditional surrender from the German army and its allies. © NARA

General Ray Barker. They were to choose the site of the future assault and to define the required resources. During the Rattle conference, held in Largs in Scotland from the 28th of June to the 2nd of July 1943, a team of fifty American, British and Canadian senior officers chose Normandy as the landing zone. The long sandy beaches, protected from westerly winds by the Cotentin peninsula, the proximity of the port of Cherbourg and the relatively weak German defences in the area were all in favour of a successful amphibious operation. It was in August 1943, in Quebec, that the date of the 1st of May was set.

Then, during the Tehran conference, Churchill, Roosevelt and Stalin finally endorsed their choice. Morgan presented the initial plans for the operation. He recommended opening a 40km-large front by launching simultaneous assaults by one American and two British infantry divisions, and one airborne division. A few kilometres separated the three selected beaches, which were codenamed Juno, Gold and Omaha.

Lieutenant General Morgan donning his SHAEF badge. The COSSAC became one of its constituent parts in January 1944. © IWM

This poster issued in 1944 aimed at encouraging the American people to purchase War Bonds, which were renamed Invasion Bonds, prior to the European landings. © NARA

A CHANGE OF PLAN

According to the commander of the 21st Army Group, if the COSSAC's plan was to be applied without modification, its chances of success were virtually non-existent. And he was not alone. Therefore, on the 19th of August 1942, in Quebec, Churchill expressed his own doubts and requested that the engaged forces be increased by 25% and that the landings include the Cotentin peninsula.

General David Dwight Eisenhower, at the time commander of operations in the Mediterranean, also carefully scrutinised the COSSAC plan that had been sent to him on the 27th of October. This officer, who had already worked for the War Plans Division and had assisted Marshall, in command of the Operations Division, immediately perceived weaknesses in the Allied plan. In his view, the front was too narrow and the forces engaged insufficient. It was essential that the deep-water port of Cherbourg be secured, for the success of the invasion would largely depend on the Allied armies' capacity to rapidly provide the necessary men and material to ensure the continuance of military operations in France.

Consequently, Ike met General Bernard Montgomery, chief of the VIIIth British Army, to discuss the plans. Montgomery was of the same view. The British general deemed the plan far too timid and doomed to result in a total fiasco. From experience, he knew that - even if weakened - the enemy remained fearsome and capable of countering the invasion. For the landing operation on the Sicily coast (operation Husky) on the 10th of July 1943, Monty had engaged a more consequential force, but the German troops posed a serious threat to the bridgeheads. In Normandy, he was in no doubt that the German forces, steadfastly

General Montgomery played a central role in the modifications to the COSSAC plan. © Rights reserved

Taken a few hours after the attempted landings in Dieppe, this terrible picture shows the bodies of the fallen Canadians being gathered together on the beach. We can also see their equipment in piles. French civilians were requisitioned to help.
© Rights reserved

The artist Dean Cornwell astutely made use of the airborne forces, considered as the elite, to collect metal. © NARA

In 1944, the Russian-born artist Boris Chaliapin represented General Dwight D. Eisenhower to promote War Bonds. © NARA

entrenched behind their coastal defences, would react even more forcefully and would engage the bulk of their divisions posted in the West.

On the 1st of January 1944, Winston Churchill read Monty's note relating his doubts on the subject of Operation Overlord. The following morning, convinced he was right, the British general set off for London with the ambition to change the plan. Once at his destination, he immediately attended a COSSAC meeting in St. Paul's School. He voiced his opinion and told the attending officers that their excessively limited plan could only result in failure.

Freshly appointed chief of the SHAEF (Supreme Headquarters Allied Expeditionary Force), Eisenhower subscribed to the point of view of the British general whom he had just named chief of the 21st Army Group. On the 1st of February, the decision was made to alter the initial plan by extending the assault sectors at both extremities. Two new beaches were added: Sword, stretching from Lion-sur-Mer to Ouistreham and Utah from Saint-Martin-de-Varreville to Sainte-Marie-du-Mont. Whereas the landings on Sword obliged the British to engage a more powerful amphibious force, those on Utah were a literal upheaval to the Allied plans.

WAS THE COSSAC PLAN TOO TIMID?

The COSSAC planners had elaborated their plan based on the available human and material resources on British soil during the second semester of 1943. In a nutshell, very little. They were totally dependent on their hierarchy to obtain figures. The Allied troops engaged in the Mediterranean and the Pacific were making use of a vast share of amphibious equipment and the number of ships and landing barges was relatively limited. The aviation's fleet of planes and gliders was barely capable of transporting an airborne division. Furthermore, the few divisions sufficiently qualified to participate in an amphibious assault were already in action in other theatres. Morgan's teams had obviously considered the possibility of a landing operation on the Cotentin shores, but they did not have the necessary means at their disposal to put their plan into action.

THE FUTURE BATTLEFIELD

This map, produced from aerial photographs taken at high altitude, illustrates the Utah Beach sector. The light-coloured zones on the edge of the beach are strongpoints. The flooded zones can be clearly seen further inland. © Rights reserved

For many within the SHAEF, the landings on Utah were a subject of uncertainty for the zone was particularly isolated and far from the other beaches. Sheltered from prevailing winds, the beach was sufficiently wide and accessible to enable both men and material to advance quickly; however, the configuration of the inland area was in no way propitious to the rapid establishment of a bridgehead.

Czech hedgehogs were originally designed for use as antitank obstacles. Even when overturned, they were equally effective. The Germans used a large number of these elements on the beaches to hinder the progression of assault barges and vehicles. © Private collection

The northernmost part of the Cotentin peninsula is comprised of rocky coastal plateaux. To the south of Valognes, the coast comprises a low plain through which the River Douve and its affluent, the Merderet, meander. The beds of both waterways are the site of vast marshlands which are, in turn, crossed by a number of drainage canals. A lock, located in the locality of La Barquette, to the north of Carentan, enables water levels to be controlled, hence drying out the marshes for the best part of the year. In the winter, the meadows and grasslands disappear under the waters. To the west, the coast is marked by a line of dunes, running from Quinéville to the mouth of the Douve. The land gently slopes upwards and inwards. At high tide, the areas located parallel to the coast that are under sea level are flooded. Utah Beach is linked to the villages of Sainte-Marie-du-Mont, Saint-Martin-de-Varreville and Ravenoville via heightened causeways of a length of one to two kilometres.

The area referred to as Le Plain is a typical bocage landscape criss-crossed by a complex network of hollow paths. The small and irregular plots of land are enclosed by high earthen embankments bordered with ditches and surmounted with hedges and trees. Villages are linked with isolated hamlets via narrow roads that run through the marshes.

The localities of Carentan and Sainte-Mère-Église, both lie along the RN13 trunk road between Caen and Cherbourg and, as such, were strategic junctions for the Allies. Their star-shaped intersections lead to the coast via Montebourg and Valognes to the north, Saint-Sauveur-le-Vicomte and La Haye-du-Puits to the west, and Perier to the south.

The Bay of Veys, into which the Aure, the Vire, the Taut and the Douve run, is a natural obstacle likely to hinder the junction between troops landed on Utah with those arriving on Omaha, some forty kilometres away.

The probability of meeting with failure was high; even higher than on Omaha. It was consequently decided that two American airborne divisions would be engaged to secure the beach exits and to take control of strategic bridges to ensure the rapid junction with troops landed by sea.

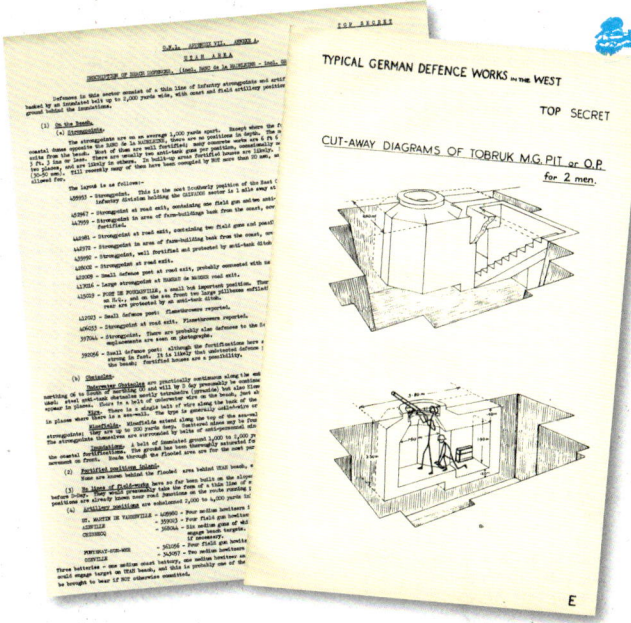

Military intelligence had close to perfect knowledge of the German defences thanks to aerial photography and to information forwarded by the French Resistance, as illustrated on these sheets detailing the organisation of the German strongpoints defending the Utah sector.
© Rights reserved

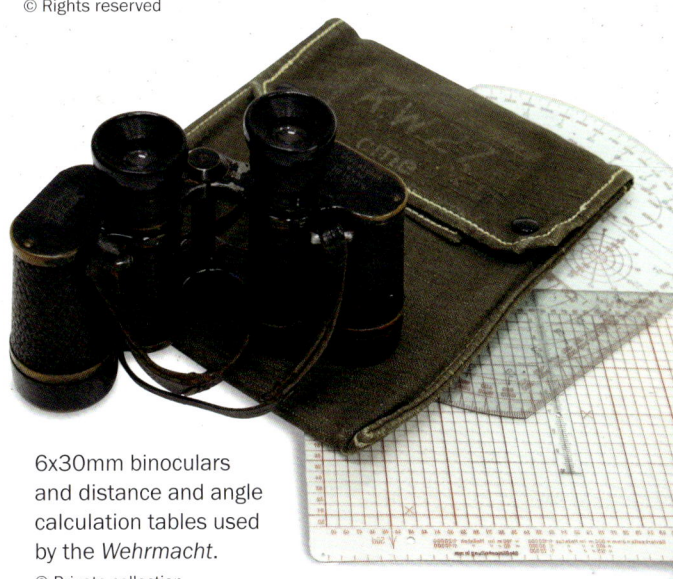

May 1944. A P-38 J fighter plane flying over the French beaches at low altitude to identify the defensive elements installed by the Germans. Week by week, the number of obstacles increased, becoming a matter of serious concern for the Allied command. © NARA

6x30mm binoculars and distance and angle calculation tables used by the *Wehrmacht*.
© Private collection

17

The C-47 Skytrain, a by-product of the DC3, became an essential tool, both for the US Army and its allies. Whereas the C-47 was the most frequently used craft during the Normandy campaign, the C-53 Skytrooper was also deployed to transport paratroops. © NARA

In 1944, the Higgins naval construction yards increased their production rate. On the 23rd of July, the issue of the 10,000th Higgins Boat was duly celebrated by the US Navy on the banks of Lake Pontchartrain. © NARA

SUPPLEMENTARY RESOURCES

The date of the landings needed to be postponed by a month in order to integrate these freshly added parameters. Planners knew exactly how many men and how much material these modifications would require. Whilst the engagement of extra divisions posed no particular problem, the same did not apply to the required transport logistics to ensure they could later reach their targets. The Allies had, since 1942, been suffering from a shortfall in landing barges. They were barely available in sufficient numbers to ensure the amphibious operations already engaged in the Pacific and the Mediterranean. To fully satisfy the needs of operation Neptune, a share of these vessels had been reallocated and sent to England. But it was still not enough. American and British naval construction yards increased their production accordingly.

The full staff of the SHAEF. From left to right: Lieutenant General Bradley, Admiral Ramsay, Air Chief Marshal Tedder, General Eisenhower, General Montgomery, Air Chief Marshal Leigh-Mallory, and Lieutenant General Bedell Smith. © NARA

Amphibious training on the American coast. The 4th US Infantry Division was specialised in this type of operation.
© Rights reserved

The Allies faced the same problem with regard to their fleet of transport planes and gliders. They were in insufficient number to transport two further airborne divisions. Early January 1944, the IX Troops Carrier Command had a grand total of one hundred C-47 Skytrain planes, barely enough to transport one airborne regiment, i.e. around 2,000 men. Twelve transport squadrons, in the form of 600 planes with crew, would consequently need to be brought in from the Untied States. The craft left Florida and headed for Puerto Rico. After stopping over in Brazil and on Ascension Island, the pilots then flew to West Africa, then to Morocco, before reaching their final destination: England. Several formations were also redeployed from the Mediterranean. By early April, a thousand Dakotas were scattered across fifteen airfields in southern England. Their crews took advantage of the remaining weeks to train at dropping sticks of paratroopers and at towing gliders.

The production line at Higgins, the firm that produced the famous LCVPs and the LCM 3s (Landing Craft Mechanized).
© NARA

HARDTACK 21

The SHAEF requested that reconnaissance operations be conducted along the coast in order, not only to glean improved knowledge of the geological and physical features of the future landing beaches, but also to perfect its understanding of the German coastal defences. Twelve operations, collectively referred to as operation Hardtack, were scheduled.

Over the night of the 26th to the 27th of December 1943, Lieutenant Francis Vourc'h and nine men from the No. 10 Commando landed on the beach at Quinéville. For around two hours, they gathered precious information on the beach obstacles, the minefields and the antitank ditch. They analysed the sand, measured the force of the current and the beach slope, then set off on their return home without being spotted.

FORCE U

VII Corps insignia. Created in 1918 and reactivated in November 1940, it was one of the US First Army's two founding elements, the other one being General Leonard T. Gerow's V Corps.
© Private collection

Major General Lawton J. Collins distinguished himself in command of the 25th US Infantry Division Tropic Lightning during the Battle of Guadalcanal. According to Bradley, the Normandy bocage landscape was as hospitable as the Solomon Islands. © NARA

Force U reunited the ships that were in charge of transporting troops towards Utah Beach and at covering the landings. The force was commanded by Rear Admiral Don P. Moon, chief of Task Force 125. Previously posted in Algeria to plan the amphibious landings in the south of France, Moon had been recalled in March to take command of Force U which, at the time, only existed on paper. This hard-working officer set up his headquarters in the port of Plymouth, part of which had been devastated by bombs dropped by the *Luftwaffe*. In barely two months, he successfully compiled a coherent naval force with several hundred ships, and prepared their crews to take control of a bitterly defended beach. Major General Collins, who appreciated Moon's professionalism, repatriated the US VII Corps to Plymouth to ensure better joint preparation of the future invasion. This close collaboration between the two army commanders proved to be highly productive.

The cruiser *USS Tuscaloosa* (CA-37) in the waters around Scapa Flow in April 1942. © NARA

After the Normandy campaign, Rear Admiral Moon was to take part in the Provence landings, but he died after shooting himself with his pistol on the 5th of August. His suicide was officially attributed to battle fatigue.
© NARA

Bradley on the front cover of the 18th June 1944 issue of the *New York Times Magazine*. © Private collection

USS Bayfield (APA-33).
The LCVPs were stowed to the side.
© NARA

THE FLAGSHIP *USS BAYFIELD* (APA-33)

This warship, formerly named *Sea Bass*, was a C3 type cargo converted into an assault troop transport ship in November 1943. Fast enough to escape the German *U-Boote*, it could transport an entire infantry division and its equipment, together with the necessary landing barges. The Coast Guard crews were placed under Captain Lyndon Spencer's command. The ship acted as the Force U flagship on the 6th of June. Both Moon and Collins were on board.

The *Bayfield* left Plymouth on the 5th of June to set anchor at 02:30 the next morning, 18km off Utah Beach. Over the days that followed, the ship was used as a command post and offered logistic support. It also served as a hospital ship and processing centre for German prisoners of war before their evacuation to England. The *Bayfield* returned to England on the 25th of June. A few weeks later, it led Task Force 87 on its way to the Provence coasts in southern France.

THE US VII ARMY CORPS

Placed under the authority of the US First Army, commanded by General Omar Bradley, the US VII Army Corps comprised the 4th, 9th, 79th, 90th US Infantry Divisions (USID) and the 82nd and 101st Airborne Divisions (AB). The divisions selected to take part in the D-Day Landings were well commanded and specifically trained. Their chiefs had all striven to offer them the necessary cohesion to ensure they withstood combat conditions. Troop motivation and morale were deemed to be excellent; however, the vast majority of enlisted soldiers had absolutely no experience of armed conflict.

Sir Trafford Leigh Mallory, commander in chief of the Allied Expeditionary Air Force, nevertheless feared that the engagement of airborne troops may turn to fiasco, due to its vulnerability to gunfire from anti-aircraft defence. He predicted losses in the region of 80%.

Servers of an Oerlikon anti-aircraft defence weapon keeping watch. In the Channel waters, the crews feared attacks by the *Luftwaffe*. © NARA

Crossing conditions were extremely rudimentary aboard the Landing Craft Infantry, which were not designed for the high seas. © NARA

Cramped inside their transport ships, the GIs killed time as best they could. © NARA

THE 82ND US AIRBORNE DIVISION

To the west, the paras from the 82nd and the 101st Airborne Divisions were to jump over the south Cotentin in order to offer protection to the 4th USID, by taking control of the access causeways towards Utah Beach. Both divisions had been engaged as airborne units in August 1942.

Engaged in March 1942, the All Americans division was behind the creation of an infantry division. At the time, its chief was no other than Major General Bradley himself. The 82nd USID was transformed into an airborne division five months later. It left Louisiana to pursue its training at the Fort Bragg camp in North Carolina. The 504th and 505th Parachute Infantry Regiments (PIR) and the 325th Glider Infantry Regiment (GIR) formed the backbone of the 82nd AB.

Over the long months, the recruits who had volunteered to serve in the army were subjected to extremely arduous military training. They were taught infantry combat techniques, learned how to jump with a parachute from a plane and accepted the idea of fighting in isolated units behind the enemy lines.

Men from the All Americans boarding the C-47 that will take them to Sicily. © NARA

Major General Matthew B. Ridgway's 82nd Airborne Division (AB) set off for Casablanca on the 10th of May 1943, securing Kairouan in Tunisia in preparation of its first operational jump. On the 9th of July, the 505th PIR was dropped over Gela in Sicily (operation Husky). On the 11th, the 504th PIR was engaged in an operation that came to a dramatic end: 23 planes were mistakenly shot down by the anti-aircraft defence weapons installed on Allied ships. The early days were laborious. However, the American paras nevertheless reached their targets and gained precious experience: the unit captured a total of 22,000 German soldiers. In September, the 82nd AB's two regiments were dropped by night in the region of Salerno (operation Avalanche). The division entered Naples on the 1st of October 1943. Colonel James M. Gavin, promoted to the rank of Brigadier General, was appointed

American knuckle duster and cicada-shaped cricket made of tinplate, used by a para from the 508th PIR in Sicily. © Private collection

THE US AIRBORNE DIVISION

The American airborne divisions were composed of three parachute infantry regiments (PIR) and one infantry regiment transported by glider (Glider Infantry Regiment or GIR), together with the customary support units. Each division comprised a total of 7,500 men, around 300 jeeps, 100 trucks, 100 mortars, thirty-five 75mm howitzers and antitank guns.

second-in-command of the division in December 1943. The bulk of the 82nd AB then left the Mediterranean front to head for Great Britain. The unit was camped in Leicester as from mid February 1944. Still in the South, the 504th PIR fought in Anzio before heading for Britain in May 1944; however, it was not due to be engaged in Normandy. Instead, on the 14th of January, the division was allocated the 507th and the 508th PIRs, in support of the 505th PIR and the 325th GIR.

Insignia of the 82nd US Airborne Division. © Private collection

In this 1942 advertisement, Winchester flaunts the light weight and easy handling of its USM1 carbine. © Private collection

Major General Ridgway with a photographer from the Signal Corps, somewhere in Sicily. © NARA

ITS MISSIONS

The plan was to drop the 82nd AB to the west of Saint-Sauveur-le-Vicomte, in order to cut the peninsula above the line of marshes. However, the site where the All Americans were supposed to engage was modified three weeks prior to the operation's launch. Indeed, the Allies had been informed by the French Resistance of the arrival of fresh German units in the sector. They comprised the *91. Luftlande Division* (*91. LLD*) and the *6. Fallschirmjäger Regiment* (*FJR6*). Refusing to send his men to certain death, Bradley decided to have them dropped on either bank of the Merderet. The mission entrusted to the 505th PIR was to take control of the village of Sainte-Mère-Église. Securing this strategic communication hub, located on the RN13 trunk road linking Caen with Cherbourg, was supposed to block any German counter-attacks and to pave the way towards Cherbourg. The 507th and 508th PIRs were to capture or destroy the bridges over the Douve and the Merderet, in order to secure the western side of the future bridgehead.

The 506th PIR at Camp Toccoa (Georgia) during the summer of 1942. © NARA

The American airborne units made repeated jumps so that each gesture became a reflex. This picture was taken in Berkshire. © NARA

THE 101ST US AIRBORNE DIVISION

101st Airborne Division insignia.
© Private collection

The unit saw the day at Camp Claiborne in Louisiana on the 16th of August 1942 before joining Fort Benning. Major General William C. Lee, the 'Father of the US Airborne', was the unit's first commander. The 502nd PIR, the original regiment, had been reinforced with the arrival of the 506th PIR. It comprised two air landed infantry regiments: the 327th and the 401st GIR. The division distinguished itself during large-scale manoeuvres in Tennessee. On the 5th of September 1943, it boarded in New York and headed for England to pursue its training. After suffering from a heart attack, Lee was replaced in March 1944 by Major General Maxwell D. Taylor, who was perfectly familiar with parachute units, for he had served as Ridgway's chief of staff. Taylor's 101st AB set up its headquarters in Berkshire and Wiltshire, where it perfected its training. In preparation for D-Day, jumps, tactical exercises and marches were intensified for these elite troops. In contrast with its sister unit, the 101st AB had no experience of combat, but its cohesion and training were deemed to be excellent.

This American poster dating from 1943 has taken the parachutist's image to encourage the purchase of War Bonds. © NARA

ITS MISSIONS

Although less experienced, the 101st AB was entrusted with securing the four heightened causeways that ran across the marshes between Utah Beach and Martin-de-Varreville and Pouppeville. The 501st and 506th PIRs were to neutralise several enemy strongpoints, to take control of the Barquette lock and the bridges over the Douve to the north of Carentan, in order to prevent any German counter-attack against the bridgehead. The 506th PIR was in charge of destroying coastal artillery batteries and in securing the two exits the furthest to the north.

Brigadier General Taylor in Carentan.
© NARA

THE USE OF GLIDERS

Qualification badge awarded to men having undergone specific Glider training or having taken part in a combat mission. © NARA

Tactical information manual for the Wago CG4-A. © Private collection

Transporting the American airborne troops mobilised the entire IX Troop Carrier Commando, i.e. 781 Douglas C-47 transport planes and 511 CG-4A Waco and Airspeed Horsa gliders. The US planners hoped to deploy the gliders at the start of the operation to quickly obtain a concentration of units on the ground. However, the discovery of vast areas covered with wooden stakes and the realisation of the great risks involved in the massive use of gliders, led to the decision not to send the 500 gliders loaded with support units, vehicles and light artillery by night.

At 04:00 on the 6th of June, fifty gliders were to transport the anti-aircraft, antitank and supply units for each division (missions Chicago and Detroit). The artillery, reinforcements and medical teams would be brought in on the evening of the 6th of June aboard 68 Waco and 130 Horsa gliders (missions Keokuk and Elmira). Two parachuted supply missions were scheduled for the morning of the 7th of June (operations Freeport and Memphis). Shortly after 07:00, the 325th GIR and other reinforcements were to be transported aboard 107 Waco and 43 Horsa gliders (missions Galveston and Hackensack). Due to insufficient gliders, several hundred troops, initially to be air landed, were finally transported by boat to Utah Beach.

Insignia worn by the men from the XI Troop Carrier Command.
© Private collection

A RATHER INEQUITABLE BONUS SYSTEM

The men who chose airborne units were paid monthly parachute jump bonuses. Officers benefited from a $100 dollar bonus, and ordinary soldiers $50. Yet the infantrymen brought in by glider received no such supplement, despite the great risks they took. Ironically, the paras only received their bonus in July 1944...

Gliders from the 101st AB with their helmet straps placed on their chins as per regulations, posing inside a Waco glider.
© NARA

View inside a Waco. To withstand the shaky landing, the men were required to wear seatbelts round their waists.
© NARA

Waco CG-4A glider. © NARA

THE 4TH US INFANTRY DIVISION

The 4th US Infantry Division, also known as 'Ivy', was the unit chosen to lead the amphibious assault on Utah Beach. This epithet was a reference to the pronunciation of the figure 4 in Roman numerals (IV). Major General George H. Cameron had an insignia bearing four ivy leaves adopted during the unit's formation in North Carolina in November 1917. The division served with distinction in France. Over 2,000 officers and soldiers were killed in combat.

Reactivated on the 1st of June 1940 in Fort Benning, Georgia, the division was transformed into a motorised unit. From August 1940 to August 1943, it took up residence in Camp Gordon, taking part in major manoeuvres in Louisiana. Then it joined Fort Dix in New Jersey. After experimenting for three years, it was enhanced with an entire infantry unit and took part in large-scale amphibious manoeuvres in Florida and Fort Jackson in South Carolina. According to its own chiefs, the unit boasted great maturity and steadfast morale. Its rather high average age of 28 is worthy of note. The troops believed they were already too old to be sent to the front lines. Yet, they left New York harbour on the 18th of January 1944 to land, 10 days later, in Liverpool. The Ivy Division was in competition with the 28th USID, which had also trained in amphibious operations,

The combatants also needed to learn to withstand fear and pain. Here we can see a GI lying across the barbed wires to enable his buddies to cross them as quickly as possible. © NARA

Pillboxes, networks of barbed wires and trenches were installed on the English beaches to best prepare the Allied soldiers. © NARA

US M1 helmet, BC-611 walkie-talkie and bayonet for Garand rifle.
© Private collection

Bradley nevertheless chose the former to take part in operation Neptune. Its new commander, Major General Raymond O. Barton, a West Point graduate, was a tough leader who took care to enforce the strictest of discipline among his ranks. The spirit that reigned throughout the unit is perfectly depicted in the Ivy's motto 'steadfast and loyal'. The 8th, 12th and 22nd Infantry Regiment were subjected to intensive training.

Brigadier General Roosevelt in front of his Rough Rider jeep in North Africa. At the time in command of the Big Red One, Roosevelt was relieved from his post, as was his commander, Allen, following a decision by Bradley and Patton who disapproved of their methods of command. © NARA

Major General Barton proved to be an excellent commander. His division was engaged in a range of theatres (Cherbourg, Cobra, Paris, Hürtgen). Barton was only to leave his position on the 27th of December 1944, due to health issues. © NARA

The 8th Infantry Regiment's 1st and 2nd Battalions would be the first to land on Utah Beach. Just like on Omaha, the infantry and various support units were reunited within the Regimental Combat Team (RCT), commanded by Colonel James A. Van Fleet.

It is often forgotten that part of the 90th USID was also engaged in the battle as early as the 6th of June. The 359th RCT was temporarily attached to the 4th USID, as was the 116th RCT on Omaha. The team was to land as from 10:00 and to secure the north flank of the bridgehead. In turn, the 8th and 22nd Infantry Regiments' 3rd Battalion was to set foot on French soil at 07:45. The other battalions would follow throughout the day.

4th US Infantry Division 'Ivy' insignia.
© Private collection

THE REGIMENTAL COMBAT TEAM

A standard infantry unit could not attack a beach and establish a viable bridgehead, for it was entrusted with a number of different missions, requiring excellent organisation and specific skills. A specialised unit was therefore set up - the Regimental Combat Team or RCT - a flexible combat unit, capable of adapting to events and sufficiently powerful to break through inland pending the arrival of the second echelon.

SUPPORT UNITS

Any amphibious operation requires the presence of support units with experience in this type of mission. Each of the four infantry battalions engaged in the assault would be covered by a company from the 87th Chemical Mortar Battalion (Lieutenant Colonel James H. Batte). Their 81mm mortars were no less than necessary to reduce the German resistance nests to silence. The 980th Field Artillery Battalion's B Battery, the 377th Anti-Aircraft Artillery Battalion and the 13th Field Artillery Observation would also be engaged alongside, as would the 65th Field Armored Artillery Battalion. Their M7 Priest howitzers would provide efficient cover by firing from the decks of the Landing Craft Tanks.

The attacking infantry would also be covered by the 70th Tank Battalion (Lieutenant Colonel John C. Welborn). They were the first independent armoured battalion to be created, on the 15th of July at Fort Meade. This hardened unit had taken part in the landings in North Africa and had fought alongside the 'Big Red One' (1st USID) in Sicily. In 1944, crews had exchanged their light M3 and M5A1 Stuart tanks for Sherman M4 Duplex Drive (DD) tanks. Thanks to an ingenious flotation system

Somewhere along the English coast, Engineers making their way through a network of barbed wire. © NARA

developed by the Hungarian engineer Nicholas Straussler, two propellers and a watertight hull, these 32-tonne medium tanks could be put to the water 5km off shore, and could make their own way to the coast.

The 746th Tank Battalion (Lieutenant Colonel Clarence G. Hupfer) would arrive with the second assault wave to offer precious support. The unit created on the 20th of August 1943 at Camp Rucker in Alabama was sent to Scotland early February 1944. The tanks that were to move through the water before reaching dry land were equipped with canvas chimneys to protect their exhaust system.

Specialised troops were also transported on site to destroy obstacles, to demine and to evacuate the wounded and the prisoners, to repair broken down vehicles, to clear beach exits and to transform the beach into a genuine logistics platform.

Activated in 1942, the 1st Engineer Special Brigade was engaged to accomplish these many missions on Utah Beach. The brigade reunited a number of engineer, signal, Military Police, Quartermaster Corps, vehicle repair and medical units, but also truck companies and port and railway battalions. The unit had also taken

M1 helmet belonging to a soldier from the 1st ESB engaged on Utah Beach. The blue semi-circle is for identification. © P. Hourblin collection

part in Mediterranean operations (North Africa, Sicily and Italy). Its commander, Colonel Eugene M. Caffey, had been temporarily replaced by Brigadier General James E. Wharton, following a tragic incident during Operation Tiger in May 1944. He was in command of over 10,000 men. The 531st Engineering Shore Regiment formed the backbone of the 1st ESB.

On D-Day, the 237th and 299th Engineer Battalions joined the eight teams of 26 sappers from the 4th Infantry Division to demine and destroy the beach obstacles in order to open breaches. US Navy units were also involved in the operation. Twelve Naval Combat Demolition Units (NCDU), each with an officer and fifteen men, looked after destroying the underwater obstacles. The US Navy's 2nd Naval Beach Battalion was in charge of ensuring communication links with the ships off shore and with the barges, of clearing the underwater part of the beach, of transferring the wounded to ships and of conducting minor naval repairs. One company was attached to each of the three battalions from the 531st Engineering Shore Regiment.

Naval Amphibious Forces insignia.
© Private collection

Insignia worn by the specialists from the Engineer Special Brigades.
© Private collection

Engineer troops used M2 flamethrowers to eliminate enemy positions. The weapon had a burn time of 7 seconds and an effective range of thirty metres. © NARA

PREPARATIONS

An Assault Team leaving its Landing Craft Tank Mk.5. These men still have their standard kit. © NARA

LCVPs and LCIs approached the beach at Street, in the Slapton Sands sector. This type of operation was absolutely essential to perfect coordination between the Navy and elements from the Army. © NARA

The units chosen to participate in the amphibious assault were subjected to intensive training. Walks, physical training, exercises, theoretical and practical lessons were maintained at a highly intense pace. Discipline was strict, for the men needed to be absolutely ready. The Ivy Division followed an intensive training programme in the Dartmoor hills in southwest England. The men's commitment was in line with the missions they were to accomplish.

Since September 1943, the American units selected to take part in the beach assault trained at the Woolacombe Assault Training Centre, where they were taught landing techniques and how to conduct their respective missions in perfect coordination with other engaged forces on D-Day. The coastal region of Devon, the configuration of which was very similar to that of the future landing zone, was used for troop instruction. Its 3,000 resident civilians were evacuated. The 30,000 men comprising Force U and who were to land on Utah Beach familiarised themselves with the landing material and techniques. Each feature of the Atlantic Wall was carefully studied in order to devise the best way to neutralise it. Networks of barbed wiring,

bunkers and obstacles were therefore built. Special equipment and explosive devices were tested.

Large-scale and highly realistic manoeuvres were organised at Slapton Sands as from December 1943, in order to perfect assault techniques and inter-army cooperation. The men were offered an opportunity to put all their recent tactical and technical instruction into practice.

The naval and air forces, service units, assault infantry, artillery and tanks were all summoned to engage in these practice exercises. The exercise codenamed 'Duck' and conducted in January 1944, offered many precious lessons. In March, two divisions joined forces for the 'Fox' exercise. From the 23rd of April to the 7th of May 1944, operation Fabius - comprised of a total of four exercises - served as the very last rehearsal. These exercises were aimed at associating all the different assault forces and at accustoming the men to assembly, boarding and landing procedures.

At last, they were all ready.

The 4th US ID and the 1st ESB taking part in a series of exercises in March 1944 in Scotland and Slapton Sands.

Muskrat I and II: 12th US IR, 1st ESB

Otter I and II: Combat Team 8

Mink I and II: 22nd RCT

Beaver: 8th and 22nd RCT, 1st ESB, 1106th Engineer Group, 502nd PIR

Woolacombe in 1944. Lines of obstacles can be seen on the beach, as can the bunkers in the dunes. © NARA

© Rights reserved

TIGER

An *S-Boot* has just launched a torpedo. © Rights reserved

An *S-Boot S-30* launched at full speed. The black panther was the emblem of the *4. Schnellboostflottille*, operating in the English Channel from May to August 1944.
© Rights reserved

General Collins was behind the plans for operation Tiger, a large-scale amphibious exercise involving Force U. The 4th Infantry Division and support units from the US VIIth Corps were positioned in the same configuration as the one planned for D-Day. Eisenhower and Bradley both attended the exercise. Boarding exercises began on the 22nd of April. On the evening of the 26th, the American troops boarded nine Landing Ship Tanks (LST). The following morning, the assault troops landed on the beach at Slapton Sands at 08:30, an hour behind schedule. The cruiser *HMS Hawkins* fired at the beach to put the men in real combat conditions. Despite all necessary precautions, several men were killed in the exercise.

But an even more dramatic incident affected Force U's preparation. At 21:45 on the 27th of April, two convoys, respectively composed of five and three Landing Ship Tanks (LST), with the 1st Engineer Special Brigade on board, left the ports of Plymouth, Salacombe, Dartmouth, Torquay and Brixham, to take part in operation Tiger. As was their habit, they sailed through Lyme Bay simulating the Channel crossing.

USS LST-289 was towed to Dartmouth on the 29th of April. © NARA

The previous day, a fleet of nine German *Schnellboote* (fast attack craft) left Cherbourg to patrol off Portland, where large tonnage ships had been spotted. On the 28th, at around 02:00, the German crews were alerted by radio of unusual sea traffic and headed straight to the sector in question. They established contact with the T-4 convoy off Portland and took up position in its wake. Cruising at 3.5 knots, the transport ships were defended by one single corvette, *HMS Azalea*, since the initially planned destroyer, *HMS Scimitar* had returned back to Plymouth after a collision with an LST.

Although the German launches had been spotted by the British radio operators, the LSTs - which were operating at a different radio frequency from the Royal Navy - could not be warned. The seamen on board heard extremely loud engines, similar to those of a plane. Launched at a speed of over 40 knots, the *S-Boote* attacked, like a pack of wolves. Far too slow, the LST were easy targets. *LST-507* was hit by two torpedoes at 02:15 and was abandoned. More explosions came a few minutes later. *LST-531* plummeted to the sea bed, whereas *LST-511* suffered damage from Allied gunfire. Despite its bow being burst open by a torpedo, *LST-289* nevertheless managed to return to Dartmouth. The search for casualties began around 05:00, but it was already too late for many seamen and soldiers, who drowned or died of hypothermia.

Victims of the operation were anonymously buried in Devon before being transferred to the Cambridge American Cemetery.
© NARA

Pair of 7x50mm binoculars belonging to the *Kriegsmarine*.
© Mémorial de Caen collection/Photo C. Prime

A HEAVY SECRET TO BEAR

The toll was known a few days later: 198 seamen and 441 infantrymen had been killed. There were 317 survivors. Later, the US Army increased these figures. During the operation, a total of 749 men had lost their lives. Four hundred and thirteen men from the 1st ESB had been killed and 16 wounded. The 3206th Quartermaster Service Company had lost 201 of its 251 men. The SHAEF was informed that 10 'Bigot' officers who were privy to crucial information on Operation Overlord were unaccounted for. The high command feared that some may have been recovered – dead or alive – by the Germans. Their bodies were found after a later search. Their secret was safe and sound. The victims of operation Tiger were hastily and anonymously buried in Devon before being reunited in the Cambridge American Cemetery. This incident was filed as a military secret. Any survivors who failed to abide by orders faced the court martial. The victims' families were only informed of the tragic truth forty years later.

THE GERMAN DEFENCE SYSTEM

A *Ringstand* or *Tobruk* was a small, open-air bunker used to house a machine gun, a mortar or a flamethrower. These weapons could also be mounted on a tank turret.
© Private collection

a signal battalion. Volunteer battalions from the East (*Osttruppen*) compensated for the transfer of battalions towards the Eastern Front. The *243. ID* was supported by a heavy machine gun battalion and a rocket launcher regiment stationed in the sector. It was offered further cover from the *Panzer Abteilung 206*, an instruction unit the majority of whose spoiled French tanks were retroceded to the *21. Panzerdivision* in May 1944.

In 1944, the Cotentin peninsula was defended by two German infantry divisions. The *709. Infanterie Division* (*Generalleutnant* Karl Wilhelm von Schlieben) occupied the eastern coast as far as Carentan and was in charge of defending the port of Cherbourg. The *243. Infanterie Division* (*Generalleutnant* Heinz Hellmich) was in turn stationed in the Valognes sector.

Each of these two static divisions comprised three infantry divisions, one artillery regiment, an antitank battalion, an engineer battalion and

80mm mortar servers during manoeuvres in the Cherbourg sector. © Private collection

Diary of an *Osttruppen* unit, and Vlasov Army (aka Russian Liberation Army) insignia.
© Private collection

The MG-34 machine gun had a rate of fire of 800 rounds/minute. Production of this high-quality weapon required 59kg of steel and 150 hours of machining and assembly. It was gradually replaced by the MG-42.
© Mémorial de Caen collection/Photo C. Prime

Given their numbers and their firing power, these two divisions were capable of leading occasional counter-attacks pending the arrival of reinforcements. The *Schnelle Brigade 30* (*Oberstleutnant* Hugo Freiherr von und zu Aufseß), positioned in the region of Coutances, was a reserve force for the *LXXXIV. Armeekorps*. Rommel had succeeded in having several units transferred to the region, including a number of engineer fortress companies, one *Nebelwerfer* (rocket launcher) regiment and two coastal artillery regiments. Several *Luftwaffe* heavy *Flak* batteries had also been speedily established in the Cotentin peninsula. Concurrently, the *Sturm Battalion AOK7* (*Major* Hugo Messerschmidt) had been positioned in Cherbourg with a little over 1,100 men.

A group from a *Fallschirmjäger* unit, taking a break near the Mont Saint-Michel, before having used any of its specific equipment. © Private collection

A Todt Organisation construction site in France. © Bundesarchiv

THE FUTURE ASSAULT SECTOR

The Cotentin peninsula was of particular strategic importance due to the presence of Cherbourg. This harbour town had been transformed into a genuine fortress and was solidly defended. It would need to withstand an attack from the sea or from inland.

As from early 1944, the French coast had been literally metamorphosed. Under the impetus of *Generalfeldmarschall* Erwin Rommel, the programme to build coastal defences had been accelerated. The foreshore had been covered with Cointet elements, Czech hedgehogs, tetrahedrons, *Hemmbalken* (wooden beams) and nutcracker mines. To the rear of the beaches, underground shelters, blockhouses housing automatic weapons and mortars, together with artillery casemates were gradually built. Minefields, networks of barbed wire and an antitank wall had all been installed to protect the area around the fortified positions and to cover dead angles.

The sector stretching from the Bay of Veys to Saint-Vaast-la-Hougue – the most propitious for a landing operation – was defended by the *Grenadier Regiment 919*, attached to the *709. ID*, in charge of the sector since January 1944. The regimental command post had been established in Montebourg. Several field batteries, installed in Quinéville, Crasville, Saint-Martin-de-Varreville and Azeville, provided support to the three battalions.

The sector was also defended by several coastal batteries, together with division artillery batteries. WN 108/HKB, installed near the village of Saint-Martin-de-Varreville, housed the *1. Batterie*, which was attached to the *Heeres-Küsten-Artillerie-Regiment 1261* (*HKAR 1261*). At his disposal, *Oberleutnant* Erben had four 122mm guns of Russian origin. The latter were installed in open-air gun emplacements, pending completion of the

The beach obstacles (*Holzfähle*), surmounted with antitank mines, were installed at a frantic pace from March to May 1944. However, the tides and the salty sea water had rendered a vast number of the mines ineffective. © NARA

With his staff, Rommel regularly inspected the Normandy coast and did his utmost to have the coastal defences reinforced. © Bundesarchiv

casemates. Further north, Azeville was occupied by 170 artillerymen from the *2. Kompanie*, attached to *Hauptmann* Dr Treiber's *HKAR 1261*. *Stutzpunkt 133* comprised four casemates equipped with 105mm Schneider howitzers. The position was endowed with an *E-Werk* shelter, ammunition holds and concrete trenches. In the vicinity of the hamlet of Crisbecq, near Saint-Marcouf, the *3. Batterie* had been installed on high ground 2,800 metres from the shoreline. *Oberleutnant* Zur See Walter Omhsen from the *HKAR 1261* was in command. The battery's original 155mm guns had been replaced by 210mm Skoda guns. With a range in excess of 30 kilometres, they swept across the Bay of Veys; however, the casemates were not yet complete. Two batteries with 105mm guns were also established in Quinéville and Crasville. Those at Pointe du Hoc and Maisy were well-positioned to cover the approach to Utah Beach.

Oberleutnant Jahnke proudly posing before a German command post, decorated with his Iron Cross. © Bundesarchiv

COASTAL DEFENCES LACKING IN DENSITY

Air reconnaissance had enabled the Allies to ascertain that the defences in the Saint-Martin-de-Varreville sector were not as dense as those in other sectors in Normandy. In theory, it would require two to three divisions to efficiently cover the 35 kilometre stretch of beach; however, the resources afforded to the *Wehrmacht* were no longer in line with its ambitions. Ideally, the space between the defensive strong points should not exceed 1.5km, but in this sector, several defences were around 3km apart, a distance which prevented them from offering mutual cover.

NATURAL DEFENCES

Hundreds of two to three metre-long wooden stakes had been planted in any clear fields likely to be used as landing grounds for gliders. The lowlands behind the cordon of dunes had been deliberately flooded by the Germans, by opening the Barquette lock, supposed to control the water level in the marshes. The 2 kilometre-wide zone was covered with a metre of water. Wide, two to three metre-deep ditches were genuine obstacles, both to men and to vehicles. Only five causeways, covered with a few centimetres of water, offered access to inland areas. The Douve and Merderet valleys were also under water.

At La Madeleine, *Widerstandnester 5* (*WN 5*), commanded by *Leutnant* Arthur Jahnke, was located at the start of a pathway. The position comprised twenty blockhouses. Combat positions were linked by a complex network of trenches and shelters. The small garrison was equipped with three mid calibre guns (under 50mm), a 50mm mortar, a tank turret and six machine guns. The perimeter was secured by means of barbed wires and a vast minefield. Jahnke was a valorous young officer. On the 20th of May, *Generalleutnant* von Schlieben decorated him with the *Ritterkreuz* for his bravery on the Western Front. *Stutzpunkt 9* (*St. 9*), located further north, was a more solid defensive position. Three 37mm turrets, two 88mm Pak 43/41 guns and four machine guns were installed over an area of 400 metres in the midst of the Varreville dunes. The strongpoint was surrounded by a daunting antitank wall. However, and despite its respective garrisons' efforts since January 1944, work was still incomplete when Rommel inspected the Cotentin defences on the 10th and 11th of May 1944.

With its four 210mm guns of a range of 30 kilometres, the Saint-Marcouf naval battery was the most powerful in the Bay of Seine, after Cherbourg and Le Havre. © NARA

The German infantry took possession of the bunkers that comprised the Atlantic Wall, in rudimentary conditions. © Private collection

FRESH REINFORCEMENTS

The *1.* and *2. FJD* were perfectly familiar with Normandy and Brittany, following several postings there from 1941 to 1942. © Private collection

Since the start of the year 1944, the German high command was fully aware that the Allies were preparing a large-scale amphibious operation on the Western European coast. Although oblivious to the precise date and location, the German generals knew that the necessary conditions for such an operation would be reunited in the spring. Time was playing in their favour, offering them an opportunity to reinforce their defences. Furthermore, it seemed unlikely that their adversaries succeed in permanently keeping their plans secret. In France, the *VII* and *XV. Armee* actively prepared to defy the invasion. News units were dispatched to the coast; a number of different scenarios were studied, in order to react efficiently and to have reinforcements brought in as quickly as possible.

In April 1944, a new threat to the Allied plans came, 10 days prior to the launch of operations. The *91. Luftlande Division* (*Generalleutnant* Wilhelm Falley) was deployed in the region around Saint-Sauveur-le-Vicomte and Valognes. Created in Baumholder on the 15th of January, the division only comprised two grenadier regiments. Ultimately designed to become an airborne division, it was as yet but a standard infantry unit, and was stationed in the centre of the peninsula.

The German high command fully intended to further reinforce the defences around the *Festung* Cherbourg. In May, an exercise during which the *Sturm Battalion AOK7* played the role of assailant by attacking between two strongpoints - precisely on the

German parachutist's M-38 helmet, parachutist gloves, gravity knife, cartridge belt, knee pads and jump insignia. © Private collection

spot where the American troops were scheduled to land a few weeks later - proved how vulnerable they were to an inland attack.

The *Panzer-Ersatz und Ausbildungs-Abteilung 100* (*Major* Bardenschlager), equipped with thirty spoiled French tanks (Renault R35 and Hotchkiss H39) had come to reinforce the *91. Lufltlande Division*, as had the *Fallschirmjäger Regiment 6* (*FJR6*). Major Friedrich August Freiherr von der Heydte, a Crete, Russia, Libya and Italy veteran, established his command post in Gonfreville. The three battalions were respectively installed in the sectors of Saint-Jores, Lessay and Méautis, to complete training for their young recruits in advance of a possible airborne assault. These young recruits were of an average age of just 17 1/2. The contingent was composed of volunteers from different branches of the *Luftwaffe*. Yet, the vast majority of its officers and non-commissioned officers were hardened Africa and Russia veterans, as was their commander.

German parachutists from the *FJR6* establishing positions in Cotentin. © Private collection

The *91. LLD* continued its training upon its arrival in Cotentin. These men from the *1058. Grenadier Regiment* are taking part in maneouvres. © Private collection

A CLOSE SHAVE WITH CATASTROPHE

In many historic reference books on the D-Day Landings, we can read of the famous *Kriegspiel* to be held in Rennes on the morning of the 6th of June. We know that the scenario for this specific 'war game' was an Allied landing on the Lower Normandy coast, accompanied with an airborne attack. Cornelius Ryan mentions this in his book *The Longest Day* (1959), as does Paul Carell in *Sie kommen* (1960). Analysis ends with this extraordinary coincidence. Yet, despite the absence of elementary sources, with a few details, we can nevertheless put forward a theory.

We know that it was *General* der Flieger Eugen Meindl, commander of the *II. Fallshirmjägerkorps*, who was behind this mapped exercise. This is why it was to take place in Rennes, for his headquarters were established in Quintin, near Dinan. Division commanders had been invited to attend, along with one regiment commander. So why Meindl? Perhaps because he was preparing for the arrival of a parachute division in Cotentin, aimed at countering a potential airborne assault. The 3 and 5. FJD were precisely posted in Brittany to lead any such mission.

The *Luftwaffe* parachute jump qualification certificate was awarded after six jumps. © Private collection

The *FJR6*, already in position in Cotentin, was in fact attached to the *2. Fallschirmjäger Division* (*FJD*) commanded by *General* der Fallschirmtruppen Hermann-Bernhard Ramcke, which was being recomposed in Cologne-Wahl in Germany following the heavy losses it had sustained in Ukraine. In

German units	Numbers	US units	Numbers
709. ID	12,320 men	82nd AB	11,770 men
243. ID	11,530 men	101st AB	14,200 men
91. LLD	7,500 men	4th US ID	10,000 men
FJR6	4,500 men	358th IR	3,000 men
Schnelle Brigade 30	1,360 men	70th Armored Battalion	700 men
Sturm-Bataillon AOK7	1,100 men	87th Chemical Mortar Battalion	370 men
Panzer Abteilung 206	385 men		
Maschinengewehr Abteilung 17	630 men		
Panzer-Ausbildung und Ersatz-Abteilung 100	665 men		

Numbers engaged in the main combat units

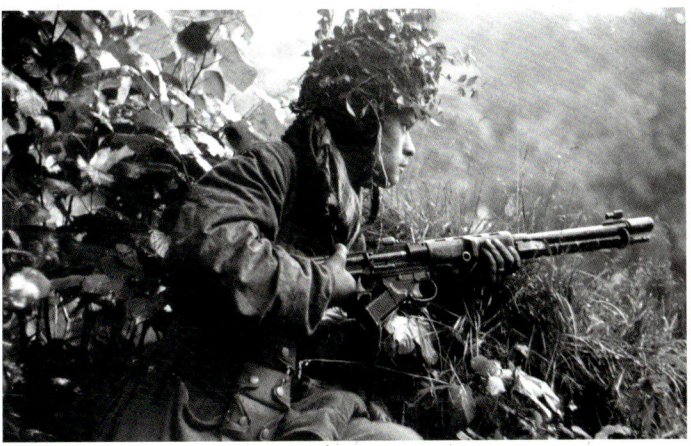

German parachute units were sent to all fronts as from 1942, to fill gaps. They were supervised by highly qualified commanders and their esprit de corps was particularly strong. © Bundesarchiv

contrast, Von der Heydte's unit was relatively unscathed and was acting as the vanguard of German presence in the zone. The German high command was most likely planning the imminent transfer of the rest of the division. The events that followed were to put stop to his plans, for the *2. FJD* was immediately dispatched to Brittany following notification of the Normandy landings. Although the unit had not yet completed its instruction period, its presence in the Cotentin peninsula would most likely have tipped the scales and rendered the task facing the US VII Corps far more complicated.

Stuttgarter Jllustrierte

STADT DER AUSLANDSDEUTSCHEN
Nr. 26 28. Juni 1944 20 Pfg.

Generalfeldmarschall Rommel während einer Lagebesprechung

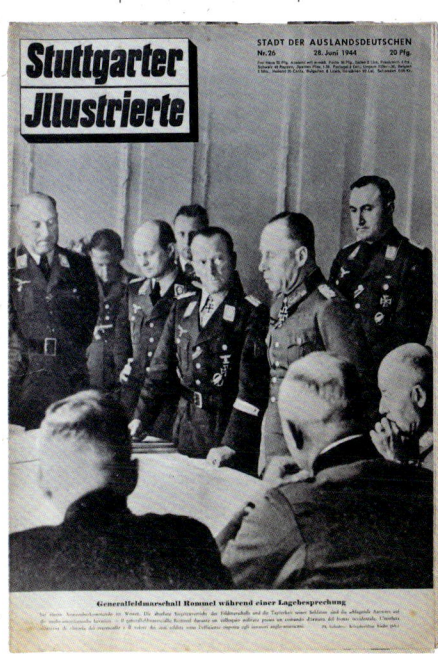

Front cover of the *Stuttgarter Illustrierte* magazine's 28th June 1944 issue, showing Rommel and Dollmann in the company of Meindl and *Generalleutnant* Schimpf, commander of the *3. FJD*. © Private collection

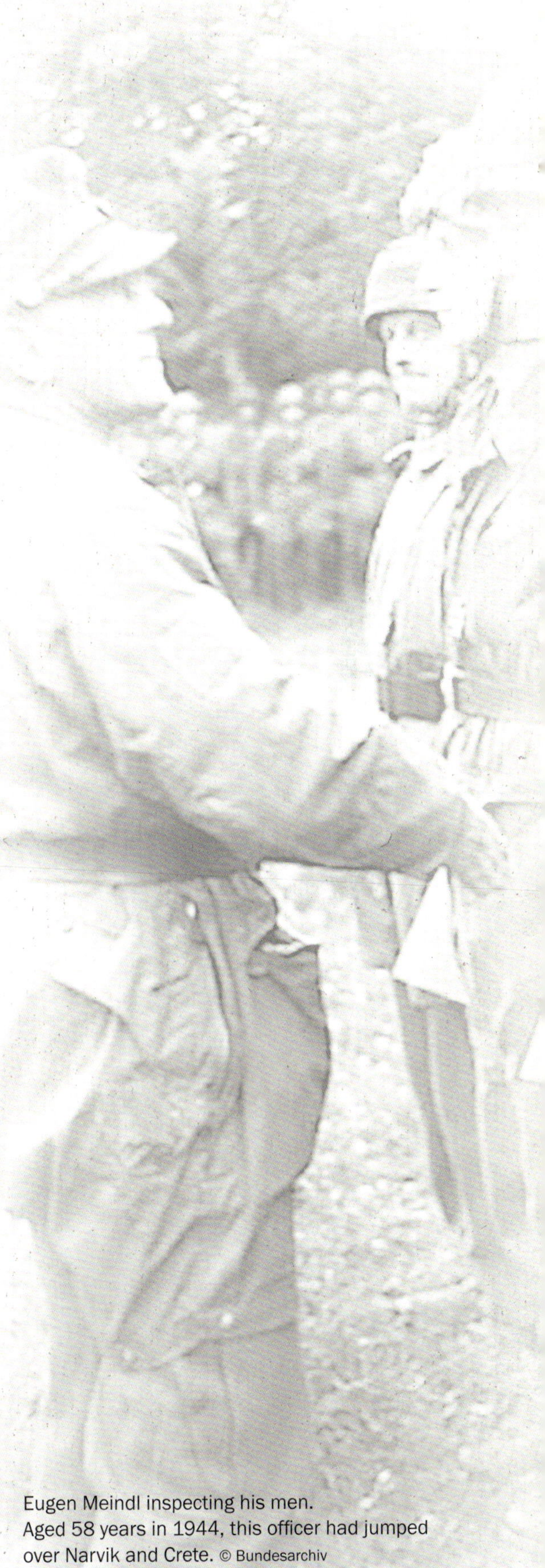

Eugen Meindl inspecting his men.
Aged 58 years in 1944, this officer had jumped over Narvik and Crete. © Bundesarchiv

THE EVE OF BATTLE

Assault Teams boarding LCVPs from the troop transport ship *USS Joseph T. Dickman* (APA-13). The ship was part of the Green Assault Group 125.4. It took part in the landings on Utah Beach on the morning of the 6th of June before returning to England to evacuate the wounded. © NARA

Men loading cases of ammunition onto a Waco glider. © NARA

Soldiers from the 90th US Infantry Division aboard *LCI(L) 326*. © NARA

Our Army magazine, June 1944 issue.
© Private collection

PART 2

THE NIGHT THE PARAS JUMPED

FALSE START

During the second fortnight in May, the land-based troops participating in operation Neptune received orders to head for their marshalling areas, near the coast. The 4th USID and attached units left the verdant Devonshire countryside, transformed over the previous months into a huge open-air military depot.

Endless convoys of tanks, trucks and vehicles of all sorts made their way, bumper to bumper, over the windy English roads. The infantry, accustomed to long marches, wore out their boots on the tarmac and along the fields that were scattered with Quartermaster Corps depots, overflowing with material, ammunition and food supplies. When they reached their destination, the men were accommodated in enclosed camps and placed under strict surveillance for an, as yet, unknown period. Their training was over; the time had come for them to wait, patiently. To avoid boredom, they played volleyball, football and baseball. Spirited card games enlivened the atmosphere inside the tents. Then - on the 3rd of June - orders, many many orders, finally came. The men rushed to their assembly points, taking with them all their individual gear. It was time to board. In the English ports, vehicles and equipment were loaded onto the barges. The perfectly tuned Allied logistics machine was ready to move into action.

Back in Southwick House, the SHAEF had been faced with deciding precisely when to launch operation Neptune. All the necessary conditions were reunited on the 5th, 6th and 7th of June: a full moon and low tide at dawn. However, the weather refused to play the game. Eisenhower set the date for Monday 5th of June. As soon as the orders had been issued, thousands of combatants took up their gear and headed for their embarkation ports. They cramped themselves inside the LCPVs that would take them to the troop transport ships. The less fortunate among them directly boarded flat-bottomed barges that would take them across the Channel by their own steam.

Force U was the first assault force to leave Great Britain, for the 865 ships it comprised were those berthed in the most distant ports of Plymouth and Poole. The ships entrusted with providing support

The utmost protection was ensured for the convoys as they crossed the English Channel. © NARA

Paras from the 101st AB gathering near their planes and gearing up before boarding. © Rights reserved

Help from a buddy was far from a luxury when attaching one's parachute harness and individual gear. ©.NARA

'Thereafter we were given a series of additional objects like a small silk escape map, a tiny compass, two hundred francs of invasion currency, and Benzedrine to help us remain awake, as well as two morphine syringes if wounded.'

Zane Schlemmer - 3/508th PIR.

gunfire left Belfast Lough late afternoon on the 3rd of June. Force U's twelve convoys gradually made their way to the assembly zone, codenamed Piccadilly Circus.

However, on the morning of the 4th of June, due to poor weather conditions in the English Channel, Ike decided to postpone the assault by 24 hours. Most of the convoys were called back to port; however, it was impossible to establish contact with convoy U-2A. The destroyer USS Forrest and a reconnaissance plane were immediately dispatched to order it to turn back. It was too late for the convoy to return to Plymouth. It was consequently redirected to Portland to join Force O. After many a tribulation, the 247 ships were finally fuelled up and could set off towards Utah Beach.

The Allied armada crossed the English Channel, preceded by fleets of minesweepers. The latter were in charge of opening channels through the dreaded minefields set up by the Germans. Seamen and soldiers all feared the sudden appearance of *Luftwaffe* bombers and *Kriegsmarine Schnellboote* based in Cherbourg and Le Havre.

Colt 1911A1 automatic pistol. © Mémorial de Caen collection/Photo C. Prime

The paras were issued with three days of K rations, along with D rations like this one in the case of emergency. Their unpleasant texture and bad taste earned them the nickname of 'Hiltler's Secret Weapons'. © Private collection

TO THE TARMAC

In the 14 British airfields, a total of 821 C-47 Skytrain and C-53 Skytrooper transport planes, together with 516 CG-4A Waco and Airspeed AS.51 Horsa gliders from the IXth Airborne Troop Carrier, waited patiently, in perfectly straight lines, for take-off. They all bore large black and white stripes on their fuselage and wings. Referred to as invasion stripes, these identification marks had been hastily painted on the Allied planes taking part in operation Neptune, in order to identify them at first sight, hence avoiding friendly gunfire, as had been the case 11 months previously during operation Husky. Any plane without these stripes would be shot down by the anti-aircraft defence and by fighter-bombers.

Mechanics and crews were busy with the ultimate preparations, as the paras geared up and headed for the planes pending orders to board. They all nervously awaited their departure. Twenty-four hours previously, although everything was ready, the announcement of the operation's postponement came. But this time, the weather was fine.

T/4 Joseph F. Gorenc from the 506th PIR boarding his C-47. This picture featured on the front page of the *Yank* magazine's 2nd of July issue. Captured on the 6th of June in Saint-Côme-du-Mont, Gorenc later managed to escape. © NARA

The M1 The M1 Thompson submachine gun boasted an excellent rate of fire and its 45 ACP cartridges offered high performance during combat, but with an effective range of only 100 metres.
© Mémorial de Caen collection/Photo C. Prime

LIEUTENANT COLONEL WOLVERTON'S PRAYER

'God almighty, in a few short hours we will be in battle with the enemy. We do not join battle afraid. We do not ask favors or indulgence but ask that, if You will, use us as Your instrument for the right and an aid in returning peace to the world. We do not know or seek what our fate will be. We ask only this, that if die we must, that we die as men would die, without complaining, without pleading and safe in the feeling that we have done our best for what we believed was right. O Lord, protect our loved ones and be near us in the fire ahead and with us now as we pray to you.'

On the evening of the 6th of June, Eisenhower paid a visit to the paras from the 502nd PIR as they waited to board. © NARA

Paras from the 82nd AB checking their gear before boarding a C-47 from the 422nd Troop Carrier Group. © NARA

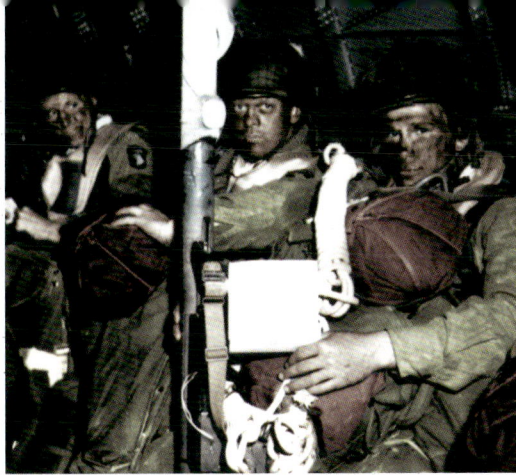
A stick from the 506th PIR F Company aboard the C-47 Dakota belonging to the 429th Troop Carrier Group that was to take them to Drop Zone C (Hiesville). Armed with a bazooka and with his face blackened, Robert Noody is ready for combat. © NARA

At 21:30, twenty planes took off and headed southwest.

They flew over the English Channel, all lights out, at an altitude of 650 feet. The planes passed over the Channel Islands and their formidable *Flak* batteries, without the slightest incident. Their 260 paras were Pathfinders, in charge of marking out the drop zones and the landing zones for gliders.

As from 22:15, 432 C-47 Skytrains took off in a deafening din from a dozen English airfields: 6,000 paras from the 101st AB were on board (mission Albany). Shortly prior to take off, the accidental detonation of a grenade damaged one of the planes, killing or wounding an entire stick from the 505th PIR. Only one man survived unscathed. The 369 craft transporting 6,400 paras from the 82nd AB followed half an hour later (mission Boston). Planes took off at 10-second intervals. Flying in formations at 500 feet, the planes strictly abode by the rules of radio silence and absence of navigation lights to ensure they were not spotted. For further safety, their route was marked out by beacons and followed by a submarine.

M-1942 jump jacket used by the 82nd AB. This wide jacket made of lightweight cotton included four flapped pockets. Due to the fragility of the fabric, the paras reinforced rub zones with pieces of heavy canvas. The Riggers in charge of repairing the parachutes and harnesses gave a helping hand. © NARA

MARKING THE DROP ZONES (DZ)

The Pathfinders were the first troops to arrive in Normandy. Most of them landed over a kilometre from their targets and had lost a vast share of their marking material. They nevertheless set off in quest of their respective zones. Marking in drop zone D (Angoville-au-Plain) was impossible for the 501st PIR teams had been intercepted by Germans as soon as they touched the ground. Their buddies from the 502nd and 506th PIRs were more fortunate and had succeeded in correctly marking out DZ A (Saint-Germain-de-Varreville) and DZ C (Hiesville). The portable Eureka transponders that would guide planes equipped with matching Rebecca radar transceivers had been installed. The Pathfinders were also to form a huge 'T' by placing Aldis lamps on telescopic tripods. The base of the letter indicated the jump direction, whereas the crossed bar marked the jump limit. Holophane lamps were of a different colour for each regiment. As for the All Americans, only the pathfinders from the 505th PIR had successfully accomplished their missions on DZ O (Sainte-Mère-Église). Meanwhile, DZ N (Picauville) And DZ T (Amfreville), together with their two landing zones, were only partially equipped.

Men from the 506th PIR 1st Demolition Section donning their war paint and Iroquois haircuts for D-Day. © NARA

A stick of 508th PIR Pathfinders posing for posterity. Four of them, including Second Lieutenant Gene H. Williams, were killed in June. © NARA

T5 back parachute harness. The paras often needed to cut its complex strap system to free themselves.
© Mémorial de Caen collection/Photo C. Prime

'As you know, I jumped at 2.30 in the morning, D-Day, landing some miles inland. The officer who was jumpmaster only knew the time limit was passed and yelled, 'Let's go!' I never saw him again. I landed all alone and it seemed like years of walking and ducking in the swamp before I ever did meet up with anyone. It certainly is a lonesome feeling being all alone behind German lines…'

Corporal Albert J. Webb
Letter dated 31st July 1944
507th PIR, 82nd AB.

As they approached the Channel Islands, the C-47 and C-53 planes took to higher altitude to escape the *Flak*. They then swerved and began their descent. As they made their final approach, the pilots returned to 1,500 feet. Strong gusts of wind obliged them to constantly adjust their flight path and their attitudes. Immediately above Barneville, the planes entered a zone of heavy fog, which resulted in dislocating their formations. The *Flak* batteries in charge of defending Cherbourg and the peninsula then entered into action. Shells and bullets hurtled though the sky in all directions. The clouds were aglow with the explosions. The formations were totally disorganised. The inexperienced pilots attempted somewhat precarious evasive manoeuvres, distancing themselves from the drop zones. Some suffered direct hits and plunged, ablaze, to the ground. Their crews had been strictly forbidden to return to England with their sticks of paras, under penalty of court martial: 196 C-47s were damaged and 21 never returned to their respective airfields.

The USM1 A1 carbine, with its foldaway stock, was specifically designed for use by paratroops. © Private collection

Each company was equipped with an optical SE-11 signal light to identify themselves to aircraft from their ground positions. However, these lamps were relatively dim and only offered efficient lighting up to a distance of 200 metres. © Vassas collection

THE TOY THAT BECAME A LEGEND

So that the paras could recognise each other in the dark and avoid any confusion with the enemy, they had been instructed to use passwords, which they were to change the following day for added security. Based on General Maxwell D. Taylor's idea, the men from the 101st AB had also been issued with small metal crickets. This children's toy made an easily recognisable, yet sufficiently discreet noise to avoid alerting the enemy. British firms were called upon to produce them in sufficient numbers and in time for the landing operation. The men attached them to their parachute straps, on the stock of their rifles or on their helmets. Certain 82nd AB units were equipped with crickets in the shape of cicadas or frogs. The All Americans had been the first to make use of them during the Sicily invasion on the 10th of July 1943.

GO! GO! GO!

© Rights reserved

'The drop was doomed to be a disaster when the C-47 pilot began to take evasive action to avoid heavy flak. He gave us the green light when the plane was in a climbing attitude as the engines roared at top speed. When I jumped, the prop blast was so severe that it tore off my pack and equipment so when I hit the ground, the only weapon I had was my jump knife.'

Lieutenant Edward V. Ott
HQ Company, 2nd Battalion - 508th PIR, 82nd AB.

To the back of the planes, Jumpmasters ordered for the paras to stand up and to attach their staticlines (automatic opening lines) to the central rail and to check their gear one last time. When the light turned from red to green, they jumped into the void, one after another, via the rear doors of the planes at a speed of over 150 km/h.

Entire sticks fell in flooded zones, whilst others - dropped too late - disappeared in the Channel waters. Tangled in their parachute straps and laden with their gear, the men drowned in barely 50cm of water. Others ended up hanging in trees or on rooftops. Some paras were even killed before setting foot on French soil. The sticks that were dropped at too low altitude plummeted down to the ground, their parachutes failing to open in time to slow down their fall. Others landed several dozen kilometres from their targets. Hence, the 3/507th PIR command

The paras were given a pouch containing a silk map and a compass to help them should they manage to escape.
© Private collection

Private Donald C. Ross from the I/506th PIR was captured as soon as he set foot on French soil. He escaped on the road to Germany and joined the Czech resistance. © NARA

The Cotentin skies criss-crossed by gunfire from the *Flak*. Due to their low speed, C-47s were easy targets. © NARA

company and a few men from the 1/501st PIR's B Company were dropped over 20 kilometres to the north of their DZ. 2nd Lieutenant Floyd R. Johnston and three other paras from the 1/506th PIR found themselves totally isolated near Pointe du Hoc.

The Germans began to hear the noise of the formidable armada of Allied planes flying overhead. In Picauville, several parachutists landed in the middle of the staff of the German *91.LLD*. The alert was raised. The Germans scrutinised the dozens of parachute canopies as they dropped to the ground. Early orders were unclear and no concerted action was possible until the Germans had a clear picture of the enemy forces they were facing, and of their targets. Small groups defied their adversaries, on the spot.

A ONE-WAY FLIGHT

The plane flown by 1st Lieutenant Sidney W. Dunagan from the 314th Troop Carrier Group was separated from its group amidst the clouds. This experienced pilot nevertheless managed to locate the drop zone. After dropping his stick of paras from the 508th PIR, he attempted a second passage over the zone with two latecomers. He was killed outright in his cockpit. His co-pilot took the plane back to base. He was awarded the Distinguished Service Cross for this heroic act. He is laid to rest in the war cemetery in Cambridge.

The isolated men who were lost in the dark hid in ditches and bushes to escape enemy patrols pending the junction with their fellow troops. The sound of gunfire echoed through the night. Men fell, knifed or shot down at point blank range. Over the early hours of the invasion, the paras had received orders not to burden themselves with prisoners. As for the Germans, certain soldiers readily executed, or even mutilated the parachutists. This was the case of the artillerymen stationed at the Holdy battery. An American patrol and several local inhabitants were also witness to the execution of seven unarmed American paras from the 507th PIR in Hémevez.

Amidst the confusion, officers did their best to gather the troops they found along their way and to head for their respective targets. Groups roughly equivalent to a 100-man section, from varying original units, silently marched through the maze of hedgerows and flooded ground. Small groups of paras erred for several days amidst the bocage landscape looking for their units and their targets, disrupting the enemy ranks on their way. Some were recovered by civilians and taken into hiding.

The 52m² canopy was opened by means of a static line attached to the back of the canopy bag.
© Mémorial de Caen collection/Photo C. Prime

The parachutist Joe Beyrle was from a family of Bavarian origin and spoke fluent German.
© Rights reserved

JUMPIN JOE'S INCREDIBLE JOURNEY

An expert in demolition, Joseph R. Beyrle from the 3/506th PIR had already accomplished several missions in France. He jumped at an altitude of 400 feet, after his Dakota had become a target for the *Flak*, and landed on the roof of the church in Saint-Côme-du-Mont. Totally isolated, he sought refuge for a few hours with a family from the village. He blew up an electric transformer before being captured. His ID tags having been found by the body of a parachutist, he was believed to have been killed. During his transfer, he escaped. However, wounded, he was captured once more. After a long journey, he was imprisoned at Stalag III-C in Poland. With several of his fellow soldiers, he escaped again and travelled to Berlin, only to be captured once more by the Gestapo. After 10 days of ill treatment, they were sent back to the Stalag, where they spent 30 days in confinement. However, nothing was to stop the impetuous US para who succeeded, one more time, in escaping from the camp. After walking for three days, he stumbled on a group of Soviet soldiers and was engaged in an armoured Guards unit. Beyrle liberated his former POW camp. He was wounded again during an airborne attack and was sent to hospital where he met Marshal Joukov. He was then posted at the US Embassy in Moscow. As soon as he was formally identified, he was sent home on the 21st of April 1945 to find his parents, who believed him to be dead. His sons followed in his footsteps: the elder served in the 101st Airborne in Vietnam, whereas the younger was appointed ambassador in Moscow in 2008. 'Joe' died a peaceful death in his sleep in December 2004 during a stay in a camp in Toccoa, where his unit had been posted during the war.

ALARM

In Cherbourg, the *Kriegsmarine* had blocked access to the port for all ships due to poor weather conditions. *Admiral* Hennecke was dining at the Villa Maurice. However, late evening, he was informed that several listening stations located between Jersey and Le Havre had detected major aerial movements. Hennecke had the *Kriegsmarine* coastal artillery batteries placed on the alert. With *Generalleutnant* von Schlieben absent - on his way to Rennes - the interim commander of the *709. ID*, *Oberst* hans Heinz Hamann, was informed of the situation. At 01:45, *General der Artillerie* Erich Marcks, commander of the *LXXXVII Armeekorps*, was in turn notified of the presence of enemy parachutists in Cotentin. Measures needed to be taken, and fast. The *91. LLD* and the *709. ID* received orders to counter-attack. Out in the field, the German troops disjointedly engaged in combat. The dispersal of enemy units was a serious hindrance to engaging reserve troops to challenge them.

These German machine gunners are waiting in ambush behind a hedge. They have camouflaged their heavy helmets with pieces of parachute canopy. © Rights reserved

THE DEATH OF *GENERALLEUTNANT* FALLEY

The commander of the *91. LLD* set off for Rennes at around midnight with *Major* Bartuzat. Informed by his staff in Picauville of the first parachute jumps, he asked his chauffeur to make a u-turn. As the car drove along the road leading to the Château de Bernaville, where Falley had established his command post, a man suddenly sprung out of a building. He was 1st Lieutenant Malcolm D. Brannen, from the 3/508th. He was in a nearby farm with 14 of his fellow troops when the car had been seen approaching. Brannen ordered for the chauffeur to stop, however, the latter tried to force the barrage, obliging the US officer to delve out of the way. His men opened fire on the Mercedes which crashed into the wall of a former flourmill. The chauffeur tried to hide in a barn but was captured. His passengers were less fortunate. Bartuzat was killed outright and Falley, wounded, was lying on the ground. He crawled to try to catch his pistol, just a few metres away. Brannen shot him dead in the head. At this point in time, these Americans were unaware that they had just deprived the *91.LLD* of its commander at a truly critical moment. It was only after the event that the Americans discovered the rank of the two German officers. Their bodies were discovered by the Germans two days later.

Jacket belonging to a *Generalmajor* from the *Heer*. Falley was promoted to the rank of *Generalleutnant* in May 1944.
© Mémorial de Caen collection/Photo C. Prime

A nurse from the 82nd AB tending to a wounded German soldier near the wreck of a glider. The bodies of his fellow soldiers are lying by the embankment. © NARA

The bodies of three fallen US paras in a ditch near Sainte-Marie-du-Mont. © NARA

At 01:30, the presence of parachute drops in Cotentin was reported to the *7. Armee* headquarters. Although the Americans were clearly seeking to isolate the peninsula at its narrowest point, it was impossible to determine the centre of gravity and the orientation of its offensive.

Generalleutnant Helmich, commander of the *243. ID*, despatched a combat group to offer support to the *709. ID*. The *Kampfgruppe* led by Müller arrived in the Saint-Marcouf sector mid afternoon. The *Panzerjäger-Abteilung 243* and an artillery battery were sent to Écausseville to offer support during the attack on Sainte-Mère-Église. *Major* von der Heydte had chosen not to go to Rennes. The same evening, at 21:15 and for the next 16 minutes, the BBC broadcast a total of 210 coded messages for the Resistance. Omen or pure coincidence - the Alsatian drivers of the regimental train had deserted a few days earlier.

At around 23:00, the *Luftwaffe* listening stations detected a large concentration of planes in the south of England. Shortly after midnight, a lookout posted in a mirador heard planes, then saw the skies light up above Cherbourg. He immediately raised the alert. The staff of the *FJR6* received a series of reports, all confirming the first. The *III. Bataillon*, camped between Carentan and Périers, was in the front lines. Its command post was attacked and enemy parachutists then challenged positions held by the *13. Kompanie*, near Saint-Georges-le-Bohon. Early combat turned in favour of the Germans. Around 60 US soldiers were attacked from the rear and captured. Southwest of the position, the *5. Kompanie* engaged in violent combat with the American paras dropped in the Raids sector, also taking many prisoners.

The paras had extra ammunition pouches taken from USAAF depots or produced by the Riggers.
© Private collection

DISPERSAL TACTICS

American airborne operations on the 6th of June. © Y. Magdelaine

The men from the 101st AB were scattered over a 40 by 25-kilometre rectangle. The 1/ and the 3/502nd PIR landed near DZ A, which had been marked out by Captain Lilyman's Pathfinders; however, the planes transporting the 2/502nd PIR ended up far from its target, dropping its stick on DZ C, originally designed to welcome the 506th PIR. Dropped too late, two sticks from A Company landed in the canal waters. Several men, including Captain Richard L. Davidson, drowned. Colonel Moseley broke his leg and left his second, Colonel John H. Michaelis, to command his regiment. The 506th faced an almost identical situation. It took the regiment's commander, Colonel Sink, over two hours to reunite the 40 men who comprised his staff.

The situation was even worse for those from the 82nd AB. The paras dropped near DZ C would not take part in the battle. The 507th and 508th PIRs, whose mission was to secure the right bank of the Merderet, were scattered across the flooded zone. For the time being, any hopes of joining forces were vain. The heavily laden paras sunk into the grass-

'As I started making my way through the field I ran into a squad of Germans. I attempted to shoot at the first one I saw, but suddenly, I felt a searing pain in my leg. The next thing I knew I was surrounded by Germans pointing rifles at my head; I thought this was the end. The German soldiers took my watch and billfold, yelled at me, and asked me if I was American. I tried to stand up but my leg would not support my weight. My captors found a stick and tied it to my leg and carried me across a field. War was a strange thing, I thought. We were supposed to kill each other, but now these enemy soldiers were looking after me.'

Clarence S. Hughart
507th PIR, 82nd AB.

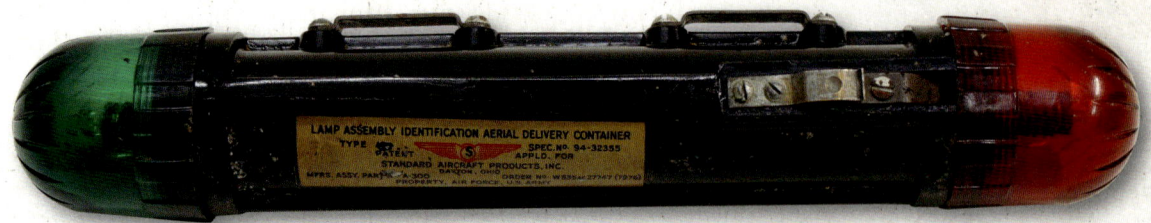

These containers are equipped with A-1 marking beacons so that the paras can find them in the dark after landing. The colour of the canopies and lamps correspond to their contents.
© Vassas collection

covered waters. Some of them, unable to free themselves from under their canopies, finally drowned. The men were unable to group together or to find their material.

Despite the glow of the moon, the coloured canopies of the containers scattered across the countryside and marshlands were impossible to distinguish from those of the parachutes that had been abandoned all around. The paras lost around 60% of their material in the marshy zones. The 377th Parachute Field Artillery Battalion was scattered at a distance of over five kilometres from its drop zone. Only one 105mm howitzer in twelve was recovered.

Captain Kenneth Johnson from the 508th PIR HQ Company walking through the village of Saint-Marcouf with his men.
© NARA

SAINTE-MÈRE-ÉGLISE
THEATRE OF THE FIRST COMBAT

Since the middle of the night, the firemen in Sainte-Mère had been struggling to put out a fire in Julia Pommier's blazing villa. A nearby barn was also in flames. Alerted by the alarm bell, the locals had rushed to the village square. They formed a human chain and passed buckets of water from the cattle market pump to the fire, under strict surveillance by the German soldiers.

Soon, they were overwhelmed by the sound of the Allied armada. Two planes with men from the 506th PIR on board flew over the village at low altitude. Parachutes opened in their wake. As the Germans on site spotted their canopies, illuminated by the flames, they immediately opened fire. The paras fell all around, in the surrounding gardens and streets. Four Americans were shot down, whereas their buddies managed to escape in the dark. A manhunt then ensued through the village streets. A stick from the 2/505th PIR was dropped on Sainte-Mère at 01:40. Alfred von Holsbeck plunged direct into the blazing house Another para was torn to shreds after a Gammon grenade exploded. Bullets hurtled in all directions and seven paras were killed before their feet even touched the ground. Their lifeless bodies hung from trees and electric poles. The troopers John Steele and Kenneth Russell landed to the less exposed side of the church. Although the former managed to free himself, the latter was captured by Germans inside the belfry.

THEN THE GLIDERS ARRIVED

At around 04:00, 89 gliders loaded with artillery pieces, anti-aircraft defence weapons, jeeps, medical teams and the military staff touched down on two hastily prepared landing zones (LZ). Although not keen to use these zones too early due to the obstacles installed by the Germans, the arrival time had been brought forward two hours to take advantage of the dark and to protect the gliders from the *Flak*.

The 52 Dakotas from the 437th Troop Carrier Group were towing the gliders participating in mission Detroit, in support of the 82nd AB. Twenty-three of them successfully landed on LZ O to the northwest of Sainte-Mère-Église, the others touching down in the fields nearby. A share of the staff, signal company, division artillery units and two anti-aircraft batteries, i.e. around 200 men, were landed. Human losses (23 wounded and 3 killed) were considered minimal; however, around half of the material had been damaged or destroyed. The paras managed to recover 11 jeeps and 8 antitank guns.

Picture taken by a para aboard a C-47, as he observed the gliders flying above the naval convoy from the window. We can distinguish the slender and aggressive outline of a battleship. © Private collection

USAAF shoulder badge worn by the Gliders.
© Private collection

Mission Chicago was aimed at bringing reinforcements to the 101st Airborne Division. A total of 52 Dakotas from the 434th Troop Carrier Group towed as many Waco gliders across the English Channel. Two anti-aircraft defence batteries, elements from the signal unit and

These men from the 325th GIR are ready and waiting aboard their Horsa glider. © NARA

engineer unit, together with a surgical team and an antitank section were transported to LZ E, near Hiesville. The fuselage housed 25 vehicles, including small bulldozers, 16 antitank guns, 11 tonnes of material and 2.5 tonnes of ammunition. The Wacos took advantage of the dark of night and landed at 04:00.

Around a dozen gliders were released too early, to land on LZ W (Les Forges), whereas six others landed on LZ E (Hiesville). The remainder was scattered across a radius of three kilometres. One crashed and the others landed near Graignes and to the south of Carentan.

Landing this type of craft in the dark, within a small and hedged perimeter, is far from simple. The gliders had trouble braking on the dew-covered grass. Their frail structures smashed into the embankments and other obstacles. Breakage was inevitable. Of the original 155, only 115 men managed to group together. Their material was pulled out of the fuselage at dawn, but the Allied troops could but helplessly observe the loss or damage of around half of their precious load, now unfit for use. Six antitank guns and three jeeps were nevertheless recovered. Only one howitzer was still operational. Minor human losses were sustained: 5 dead, 24 wounded or unaccounted for. Much to Taylor's regret, the glider carrying the powerful SCR-499 radio that was to enable him to communicate with England had been forced to return to its base.

From 21:00 to 23:00, new trains of gliders made their approach. This time, substantial resources were involved. The operation was so perilous that the LZs were under direct threat from entrenched German troops in the nearby hamlets. Ridgway was informed and immediately ordered for the craft engaged in mission Elmira to reroute towards LZ O which, in the meantime, had been secured

The waltz of gliders continued above LZ E in Hiesville, on the 7th of June. The presence of tanks on the road suggests that, at this point in time, the zone had been secured. © NARA

This Horsa has successfully landed. The presence of grid ramps indicates that a jeep has been effortlessly unloaded from the craft. © NARA

A hedge marks the end of the road for this Waco glider. The state of the structure illustrates how violent the crash must have been. © NARA

This Horsa glider transporting men from the A/325th GIR has overturned after hitting large trees during its approach. Eight of its occupants were killed in the crash. © NARA

by the 505th PIR. However, the pilots continued in the same direction, towards LZ W, where 140 Horsa gliders and 36 Wacos were to land in four successive waves, with some 1,190 men from the 82nd AB, 67 jeeps, 24 105mm and 75mm howitzers, 13 antitank guns and 55 tonnes of equipment. Small groups of German soldiers infiltrated the landing zone and opened fire on the gliders. The pilots, who had undergone intensive training, retaliated like simple infantrymen. No less than 227 men, among whom 26 pilots, were killed or wounded. One C-47 and five gliders were destroyed, 92 others damaged.

Meanwhile, the 32 Horsa gliders engaged in mission Keokuk began their descent towards LZ E: 40 vehicles, 19 tonnes of equipment, 6 antitank guns and 157 troops from support units were on board. These craft were also the target of German gunfire; however, fewer losses were sustained compared to Elmira.

ARRIVAL OF THE LAST ECHELONS

The 325th GIR and the last support units from both divisions arrived the following day with 2,300 men. The 152 Wacos and 28 Horsas engaged in missions Galveston and Hackensack began to land on LZ W as from 07:00. They lost 205 men in the process. Due to the lack of pilots and gliders, several hundreds of glider units were brought in by boat over the afternoon. Often considered as the poor relations of the airborne army, the gliders nevertheless succeeded in accentuating pressure on the German troops. The last reinforcements arrived by air on the morning of the 7th of June (mission Freeport).

Fixation system for a Waco glider.
© Private collection

THE FIGHTING FALCON'S TRAGIC END

The Fighting Falcon, a Waco glider, was flown by Lieutenant-Colonel Mike Murphy. This 37 year-old senior glider pilot had served as a civilian test pilot. By his side, 2nd Lieutenant John M. Butler, was his co-pilot. Their mission was to take Brigadier General Don F. Pratt, second in command under Taylor, of the 101st AB, to his destination. Pratt was initially supposed to land with his glider units on Utah, but his superiors had finally authorised him to arrive by air. 1st Lieutenant John L. May was by his side. Despite making a perfect landing, the Waco - heavily laden with the weight of the jeep and signal equipment - skidded on the damp grass and crashed into a nearby embankment. The glider was no more than a mass of steel tubes, of wood and canvas. Murphy lay, seriously wounded, amidst the debris. Butler, the co-pilot, had been killed by the branch of a tree that had pierced through the cockpit. Pratt, who was sitting in the jeep, was killed outright, his neck broken. On the back seat, May came out of the accident unscathed. The Brigadier General's death was a terrible blow to the 101st AB.

CAPTURING SAINTE-MÈRE-ÉGLISE

Thanks to the pathfinders, 75% of the 505th PIR's sticks landed in or close to DZ N, located to the east of the flooded zone around the Merderet. Lieutenant-Colonel Edward Krause, in command of the 3/505th PIR, landed with his stick within 1,600 metres of the village of Sainte-Mère-Église. He sent his men to search the nearby countryside looking for lost troops. He was told by a wine-laden local that part of the garrison had left Sainte-Mère. Forty-five minutes later, the officer marched towards the village with a quarter of his battalion. The paras entered and took control of the sleepy locality. At around 04:30, thirty or so Germans were captured 'in their beds or outside', and eleven were killed. The survivors retreated to Fauville. Krause had the telephone line linking Sainte-Mère with Cherbourg cut and had roadblocks positioned to the east and the west of the village; however, no courrier managed to locate Colonel Ekman to inform him that the locality was under Allied control.

Lieutenant Colonel Benjamin Vandervoort, commander of the 2/505th PIR, had succeeded in reuniting 575 of an original total of 630 men. With a broken angle, the officer undertook to head for the north of the village to establish roadblocks and to fend off any counter-attack. However, convinced that the enemy still occupied the village, Ekman ordered for Vandervoort to halt his plans. After a series of orders and counter orders, the regiment finally resumed its progression.

Private Elmet Habbs taking a rest at the foot of the sign at the entrance to the village of Sainte-Mère. © NARA

The wreck of a *Sturmgeschutz III* assault gun lying on the roadside on the road to Neuville-au-Plain. It was destroyed by an antitank gun or a baz during the attack on the *GR. 1058*. © NARA

At 09:30, the Star-Spangled Banner that had been used by the regiment during the Naples operation was hung on the façade of the village hall. At that very instant, German shells showered down on Sainte-Mère: five *Panzer* tanks and two *Ost Batallion 795* companies were attacking from the south. The paras were given a rough time, sustaining minor losses. However, an antitank gun put several tanks out of action, obliging the assailants to withdraw to Fauville.

Mid morning, 1st Lieutenant Turner Turnbull's D Company platoon established a roadblock on

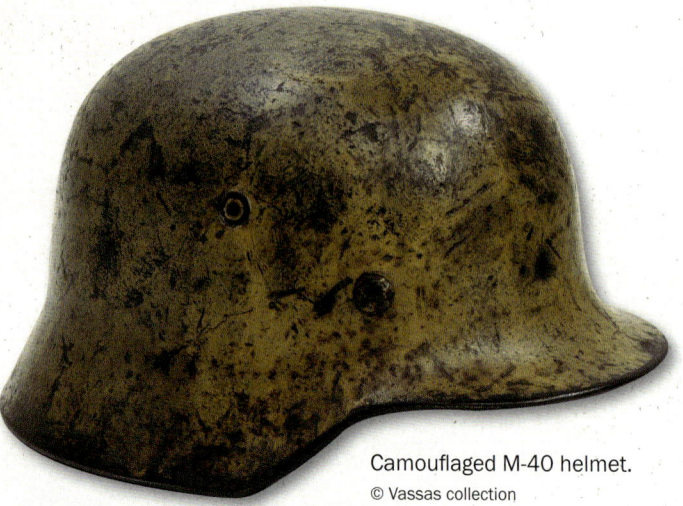

Camouflaged M-40 helmet.
© Vassas collection

the RN13 trunk road level with Neuville-au-Plain. At the age of just 22, the officer was in command of 42 men, one 30 calibre machine gun, several FM Bar automatic rifles, a bazooka, a 60mm mortar and a 57mm gun. With tank support, the platoon challenged an infantry battalion from the 91. LLD. After eight hours of combat, Turnbull and 16 other escapees retreated, leaving the seriously wounded behind. The same evening, 356mm shells fired by the cruiser USS Nevada showered down on the Neuville-au-Plain sector, putting a permanent end to the German offensive north of Sainte-Mère. The young officer, nicknamed 'The Chief' by his men, because of his American Indian origins, was killed the next day.

The Niland brothers. © Rights reserved

FROM FICTION TO REALITY

The film Saving Private Ryan by Steven Spielberg, tells the story of the rescue of a parachutist from the 101st AB by a team commanded by an officer from the 2nd Rangers Battalion, Captain John H. Miller, played by Tom Hanks. Although the story and the characters are fictional, the film is based on the true story of the Niland brothers from the State of New York.

The eldest brother, Edward, a Technical Sergeant in the USAAF, was reported missing in the Pacific on the 16th of May 1944. His three brothers were all engaged in Normandy. Preston, 2nd Lieutenant in the 22nd IR's 1st Battalion, landed on Utah Beach on the 6th of June. The youngest brother, Frederick Fritz, enlisted in the 501st PIR, had been dropped a few hours earlier. Technical Sergeant Robert Niland, from the 505th PIR, fought alongside 1st Lieutenant Turnbull at Neuville-au-Plain. He was killed behind his machine gun as he covered his unit's retreat. Preston was killed the following day during the attack on the Crisbecq battery.

Considered as the last surviving Niland brother, Frederick was sent back to the United States, where he served in the Military Police until being demobilised. He later found his elder brother Edward, who had in fact been taken prisoner by the Japanese. Preston and Robert Niland's bodies are buried side by side in the Normandy American Cemetery in Colleville-sur-Mer.

LA FIÈRE

The 82nd AB's second objective was to establish a defensive position to the west of the Merderet and to capture the two bridges over the river. Groups of paras also converged towards the La Fière sector. An initial assault was launched immediately after daybreak, but - due to the marshes - the Americans were forced to advance along the causeway leading to the bridge. They were stopped by machine gunfire coming from a nearby manor, where thirty Germans were entrenched. Major contingents from the 507th and the 508th PIRs, dropped to the east of the river, had nevertheless succeeded in joining forces at their target. Mid morning, around 600 soldiers were gathered to the south of La Fière, commanded by Colonel Lindquist from the 508th PIR. Around midday, three companies set off towards the bridge, where they neutralised the German defenders. The Americans could now set foot on the west bank of the Merderet.

A few hundred metres further west, Colonel George van Millett and around forty paras from the 507th PIR engaged in combat with the Germans occupying the village of Amfreville. Alerted by the shooting, Timmes and thirty paras attacked to the east; however, enemy fire was so intense that they were forced into retreat. They established a defensive position in an orchard on the edge of the marshes. Captain Floyd B. Schwarzwalder was sent to Cauquigny, a strategic control point on the road towards La Fière. Millett took up position in the hamlet of Les Landes.

This young German 80mm mortar server was killed seated at the foot of an embankment. His body was painstakingly scrutinized by the paras in search of documents or useful spoils.
© NARA

German case for storing 80mm mortar shells.
© Private collection

Early afternoon, 200 grenadiers from the *GR. 1057* overwhelmed the paras, isolating Timmes and his men. The Germans accentuated the pressure on the La Fière bridge, which was held by a 505th PIR battalion. At around 16:00, the US paras defending the La Fière position saw them approach, led by three R-35 tanks belonging to the *Panzer-Ersatz-Abteilung 100*. The American positions were showered with shells. Soon, A Company only had fifteen men still fit for combat. The servers of the 57mm antitank gun that was defending the causeway were put out of action. Led by Sergeant Owens, the survivors steadfastly held their positions and even managed to destroy the tanks with a bazooka. The enemy requested a 30-minute truce to recover its wounded men, before bringing a halt to the attack. The arrival of around a hundred men from Chef-du-Pont was to stabilise the situation by evening.

The Germans engaged extensive resources to keep hold of the hamlet of Cauquigny, the only access route across the marshes to the west. Two paras posing in front of the chapel immediately after the combat ceased. © NARA

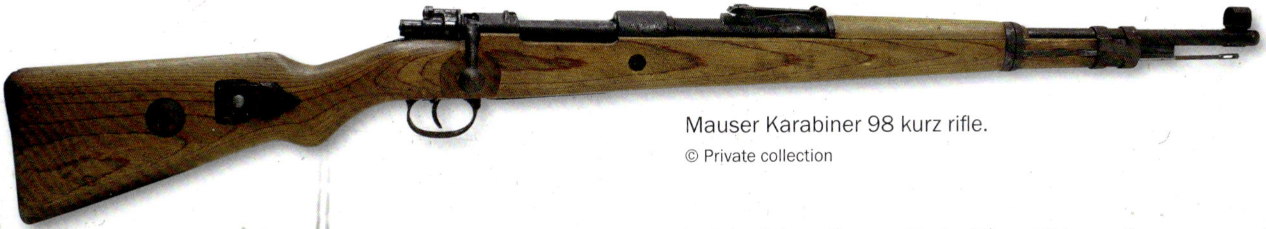

Mauser Karabiner 98 kurz rifle.
© Private collection

In this picture, the road to La Fière still bears the scars of the furious combat waged on the 6th of June. The wrecked tanks are of French origin, spoiled by the Germans and put out of action by the US paras. © NARA

CHEF-DU-PONT

The 1/505th PIR was entrusted with capturing Chef-du-Pont. The latter having advanced towards La Fière, General Gavin requested that Lieutenant-Colonel Arthur A. Maloney's 3/507th PIR find a different bridge over the river, then sent the 1/507th PIR, commanded by Lieutenant-Colonel Edwin J. Ostberg to take control of the locality and its precious bridge. However, they had neglected the presence of Germans, solidly entrenched on either side of the waterway. Ostberg was wounded in the very first minutes. A gun positioned on the right bank caused losses in the American ranks. Both sides received reinforcements and intense close-range combat ensued. Alerted by the noise of the battle, Maloney adopted a hastier pace to lend a hand, but received orders from Gavin to head for La Fière. After an ultimate counter-attack, the Germans withdrew by night towards Carquebut. The sector was finally secured with the arrival of a hundred or so infantrymen from the 8th IR.

A para from the 501st PIR keeping a German soldier at bay. The American is armed with a bayonet, a stick grenade and a German fibre flask. © NARA

A grenadier waiting in ambush and keeping a close watch over the surrounding landscapes thanks to his binoculars. Danger could strike at any time. © Private collection

HILL 30.

Lieutenant Colonel Shanley, in command of the 2/508th PIR, marched towards Pont-l'Abbé, leading a troop of 300 paras. Since his column was unable to find another bridge to cross the Merderet, the officer took position on hill 30. This isolated promontory in the middle of the marshes was located to the north of the causeway leading to Chef-du-Pont, and was in the immediate vicinity of the *91. LLD* command post. The Germans attacked the paras' positions, but failed to dislodge them. A support column sent by Colonel Roy E. Lindquist reached the opposite bank before being stopped in its tracks. The paras set up a barrage on the road but, on the 8th of June, a violent counter-attack forced them to retreat to the east bank of the Merderet. The situation had become critical. Shells plummeted down on Shanley and his men, whose food and ammunition supplies were dwindling. A patrol of 23 parachutists led by 1st Lieutenant Woodrow W. Millsaps succeeded in securing the area on either side of the road, hence enabling a convoy to bring in fresh supplies. The road was nevertheless still subjected to enemy gunfire. It was only on the 10th of June that reinforcements reached Shanley's group and permanently drove the German troops out of Picauville.

A column of German prisoners duly escorted to the coast to be evacuated. © NARA

M1 Garand rifle cartridge belt and Taylor liquid-filled wrist compass. © Private collection

The *Artillerie Regiment 191* field batteries in position around Sainte-Marie-du-Mont were equipped with 105mm Leichte Feldhaubitze FH18/40 howitzers similar to this one.
© Private collection

Captain Kenneth L. Johnson from the 508th PIR, HQ Company talking to two French civilians in Saint-Marcouf. This picture was published in several American newspapers. © NARA

SAINTE-MARIE-DU-MONT

The Germans had installed three batteries, each with four 105mm howitzers within the territory around the village of Sainte-Marie-du-Mont, occupied by around sixty soldiers from the *Artillerie-Regiment 191*. As per the established plan, the 506th PIR and the 3/501st PIR were to land on drop zone C, located a kilometre to the east.

However, the drops did not go according to plan. Throughout the night, the paras were dropped within or close to the village. As they made their descent, the Germans fired from all directions. Groups of landed paras meandered through the dark streets. One of them took refuge behind a water pump and shot down several enemy soldiers. Near the war memorial, one para and one German shot each other at point blank range. Non-commissioned officers David B. Rogers and Issac Cole from the 1/506th PIR headed for the church belfry.

One kilometre from Sainte-Marie-du-Mont, a stick from the 1/506th PIR's HQ Company landed in the vicinity of the Holdy battery. The men who had not been killed suffered horrific torture, before being massacred by the German artillerymen. In the morning, Captain Lloyd Patch took the position by surprise with 70 men, but failed to drive out the entrenched German gunners. Fresh reinforcements enabled Captain Knut H. Raudstein to resume the assault. The German defenders put up bitter resistance until bazooka fire forced them to surrender. By precaution but with regret, Colonel Sink destroyed four guns he had hoped to be able to use against their former owners.

Waterproofed M-1936 Musette bag found in the attic of a house in Pouppeville. Traces of a phosphorescent disc sewn onto the flap confirms that it belonged to a US para.
© Private collection

American paras making their way through Saint-Marcouf. This black-faced Technical Sergeant is sitting on the rubble, suggesting the sector is now calm. Yet, the men stayed permanently on the alert. © NARA

Another cunningly camouflaged battery located on the side of a hedge near the manor in Brécourt had escaped the Allies' attention. Lieutenant-Colonel Robert L. Strayer from the 2/506th PIR, whose mission was to secure Exit 2, had only managed to reunite around 100 of his battalion's original 600. He asked for E Company to look after the Brécourt guns that had been firing on Utah since dawn. In the absence of the company's leader, Captain Meehan, the attack was led by 1st Lieutenant Richard D. Winters, accompanied by a dozen men. The C-47 Skytrain with Captain Thomas Meehan and his stick on board had crashed near Beuzeville-au-Plain.

Covered by 30 calibre machine guns, the two groups, led by Lieutenants Winters and Compton infiltrated the maze of trenches between the artillery pieces. The suddenness of the attack took the German gunners totally by surprise and they put up but feeble resistance. Their guns were put out of action, but the remaining Germans still inside the manor retaliated and it was finally the US paras who were forced into retreat. Four of them were killed and two wounded. Among the German ranks, there were fifteen dead, 20 wounded and 12 prisoners. This astutely devised assault earned Winters the *Distinguished Service Cross*.

105mm shell holders.
© Private collection

GAINING CONTROL OF THE CAUSEWAYS

With support from the 377th Parachute Field Artillery Battalion (PFAB), the 502nd PIR was in charge of securing Exits 3 and 4, and of neutralising a battery armed with 122mm Russian howitzers. Lieutenant Colonel Robert Cole's group reached Audouville-la-Hubert and entrenched themselves in the concealed area inland from Exit 3. Lieutenant-Colonel Patrick F. Cassidy's group headed for the locality of Mézières, most likely occupied by the gunners from the Saint-Martin battery. The farm 'W' was devoid of enemy troops and the paras could establish roadblocks between Beuzeville and Foucarville, before advancing as far as the battery located in La Croix aux Bertots, also deserted. The Germans had moved the guns elsewhere for safe shelter. Only the wreck of one gun, destroyed during a bombardment, had been left behind. Cassidy's group took control of the village, where he found Lieutenant-Colonel Steve A. Chapuis - wounded in the leg - and a dozen other paras.

The last remaining Germans defending their strongpoints gradually ceased fighting. Whilst some had no other choice but to surrender, others rushed to the rear via the causeways, unaware that the American paras were expecting them at the other end. Ambushes destroyed several convoys and columns as they rushed out of the beaches. Hence, Cole and his men put over 50 German troops out of action.

In the evening, men from the US Navy watched the glider formations fly overhead. © NARA

The Marmion farmyard, controlling the road that led to the beach, became an assembly zone for the Screaming Eagles, who had been scattered around Ravenoville. © NARA

A group composed of men from the 502nd and the 506th PIRs, led by Major John P. Stopka, was on its way to Ravenoville. At the southern extremity of the village, the paras were stopped in their tracks near the Marmion Farm, where the *GR. 919*'s *4. Kompanie* had established its command post (*WN 11a*). The position controlling the road leading

The strength and reliability of the Browning HP 35 semi-automatic handgun were greatly appreciated by the German parachutists.

© Private collection

Captain Johnson's group taking a break in the village of Ravenoville. © NARA

An MG 34 machine gun on a Lafette 42 tripod serving in a field battery. © Private collection

to the beach was attacked. Around thirty Germans were killed or captured. Over the hours to follow, the farm became an assembly point for lost paras.

After ensuring the causeways were now safe, Cassidy established defensive positions to the north and south of Farm W, then sent a patrol to target XYZ, a group of farms and barns located along the road at the exit of the Les Mézières hamlet. The Americans failed to chase out the Germans entrenched in the sturdy stone buildings. Staff Sergeant Harrison Summers cleared around ten buildings with just a submachine gun and grenades. The eleventh, which housed a vast share of the garrison, was burnt down by bazooka fire. The Germans fled under Allied crossfire. Over a hundred Germans were killed and thirty taken prisoner.

Cassidy sent another patrol on a reconnaissance mission to Exit 4, still subjected to German artillery fire. The village of Beuzeville-au-Plain was liberated in the afternoon. The paras from the 502nd PIR installed several roadblocks around Fourcarville, whilst sustaining repeated attacks throughout the day.

Further south, three battalions from the 506th and the 501st PIRs were in charge of Exits 1 and 2, where they encountered staunch resistance. Dropped far from its DZ, Lieutenant-Colonel Robert L. Strayer's group of 200 men was to reduce to silence a number of resistance nests before heading for Exit 2 early afternoon. The first elements landed had already advanced inland. At the same time, Captain Lloyd E. Patch and his men took control of Sainte-Marie-du-Mont.

Concurrently, Lieutenant-Colonel Julian Ewell from the 3/501st PIR reached the Hiesville sector and set up the division command post. He marched towards Pouppeville at around 06:00 with forty men. The hamlet was occupied by around sixty grenadiers from the GR. 1058. Although in lesser numbers, the assailants cleared the houses one after another and took full control of the locality at around 11:00 after fighting for three hours. Taylor, who had no idea of the situation his troops were in, advanced with a detachment towards Pouppeville, at the outlet of Exit 1.

The Holdy battery suffered greatly from the bombardments. © NARA

LA DOUVE

The 3/506th PIR had been entrusted with the mission of protecting the south flank by capturing the two bridges over the Douve, built by the Germans near Brévands, in the locality of Le Port. Unfortunately, the sticks were scattered over a large zone and many paras had been killed under German gunfire from the *GR. 915* whose men were waiting for them on solid ground. Only fourteen men succeeded in reaching the assembly point, where they waited in vain for their officers to arrive. Lieutenant-Colonel Wolverton, his second in command and three company commandos had

101st AB and Technicial Corporal rank badges. © Private collection

Men from the 502nd PIR enjoying a moment's respite and a K ration at the locality of La Gouderie in Angoville-au-Plain. Jack Wormer, from Lieutenant Charles Mellen's demolition platoon, is seated on the right. © NARA

also been killed or taken prisoner. A small group led by Captain Charles G. Shettle managed to reach the bridges at around 04:30. They crossed the waterway and reduced the enemy positions to silence; however, the German reaction forced them to rejoin forces with their fellow soldiers on the opposite bank. Nevertheless, the unexpected arrival of around forty men enabled Shettle to maintain his position. A little later, a new assault offered him a foot on the right bank of the Douve.

T5 chest parachute. The stencilled letters RS indicate that it was used by a para from the 506th PIR.
© Mémorial de Caen collection/Photo C. Prime

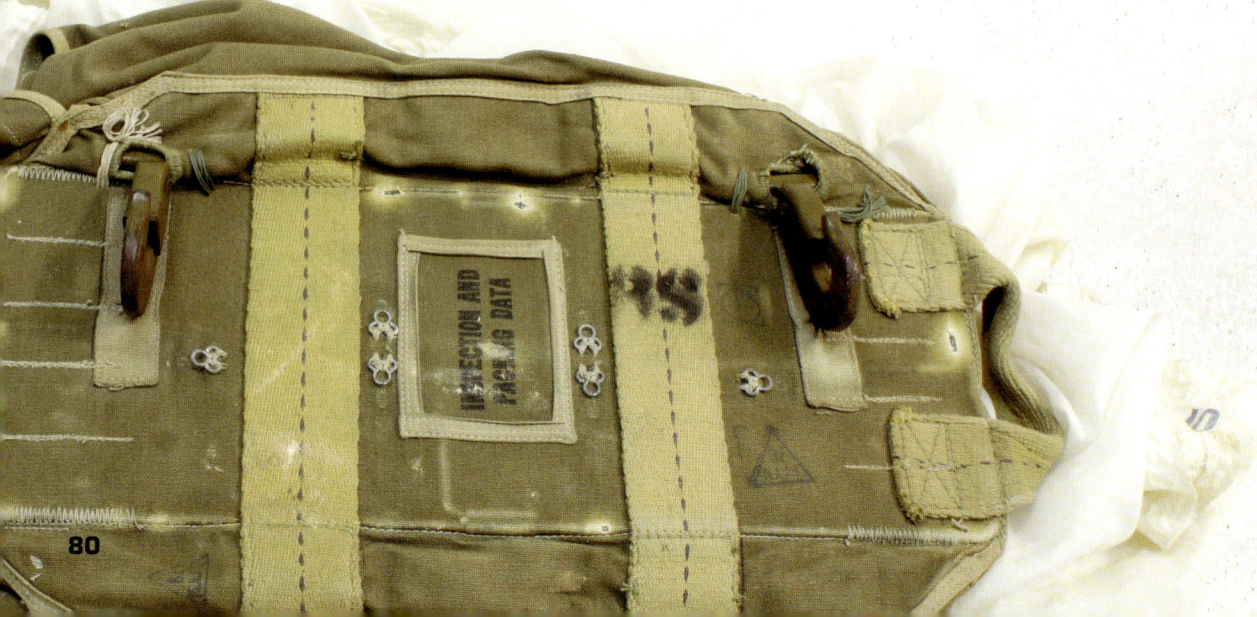

The 501st PIR was in charge of seizing the Barquette lock controlling the water level and of protecting the south flank. Two-thirds of Lieutenant-Colonel Robert C. Caroll's 1/501st PIR landed on or close to DZ D. However, the battalion was devoid of a commanding officer, Caroll having been killed and his second taken prisoner. No other ranking officers could be found. Thankfully, Colonel Howard R. Johnson reunited 150 men and launched the attack, but the German artillery was quick to retaliate. The German shells showered down on the sector all day long. Johnson organised his position to the south of the lock. Salvoes from the 203mm guns aboard the heavy cruiser USS Quincy helped reduce the intensity of the German gunfire. Combat continued the following day. Meanwhile, the 2/501st PIR was subjected to violent resistance to the east of its targets, Saint-Côme-du-Mont, the railway line and the bridges over the RN13 trunk road.

Bodies of men from the *Fallschirmjäger*, most likely those killed at La Barquette, cramped into a GMC to be transported for burial. The officer is a Captain (*Hauptmann*). © NARA

CONTACT WITH THE *FALLSCHIRMJÄGER*

Although the *FJR6* was comprised of very young recruits, their commanding officers succeeded in establishing sufficient cohesion in barely a few weeks.
© Bundesarchiv

It was in the sector around Saint-Côme-du-Mont and the River Douve that the fighting was the most perilous. During the best part of the night, elements from the *709.ID* and the *FJR6* were a permanent threat, engaging the paras from the 101st AB. At dawn, Von der Heydte received orders to launch a counter-attack between Sainte-Mère-Église and Carentan. He reorganised his forces from his command post established in Saint-Côme-du-Mont. The *II. Bataillon* (*Hauptmann* Mager) was sent to Turqueville to protect the regiment's left flank. The *I. Bataillon* (*Hauptmann* Preikschat) moved towards Sainte-Marie-du-Mont to attempt a junction with the men from *WN 5*. As they approached the locality, the German parachutists were welcomed by intense gunfire. Deprived of communication links and short of ammunition, Preikschat decided to surrender, but small groups nevertheless tried to reach Carentan via the Douve marshes. Johnson's men opened fire just 350 metres from the escapees. After an hour and a half of intense gunfire, they obtained the surrender of the decimated German ranks. The Americans had lost 40 men (10 killed and 30 wounded), whilst around 150 Germans had been put out of action. Only 25 *Fallschirmjäger* managed to join their lines. The battalion was literally annihilated. The *III. Batallion* (*Hauptmann* Trebes), left in reserve, crossed the Douve in an attempt to restore links with the *I. Bataillon*, but its progression was rapidly stopped by the Americans.

The Allied armada approaching the Normandy coast. © NARA

PART 3

THE AMPHIBIOUS ASSAULT

THE NAVAL BOMBARDMENT

The deck of *USS Hobson* cluttered with around a hundred cartridge cases. © NARA

Force U's mission was to neutralise the strongpoints and artillery batteries that were a threat to Utah. The warships comprising the force advanced via seven channels opened by fleets of minelayers. The four troop transport ships anchored 18 kilometres off shore, out of range of the Crisbecq and Saint-Marcouf guns. *USS Nevada*, along with the cruisers and destroyers, were poised off Utah Beach as per the Allied plans. Each ship had been entrusted with several specific missions. They would then opportunely deal with all the attainable targets that presented themselves throughout the day.

Composition of Force U

Battleship: *USS Nevada* (BB-36)

Heavy cruisers: *USS Tuscaloosa* (CA-37), *USS Quincy* (CA-71), *USS Hawkins* (DD-873),

Light cruisers: *HMS Black Prince* (81)

Destroyers: *USS Butler* (DD-636), *USS Corry* (DD-463), *HMS Enterprise* (D52), *USS Fitch* (DD-462), *USS Forrest* (DD-461), *USS Glennon* (DD-620), *USS Herndon* (DD-638), *USS Hobson* (DD-464), *USS Jeffers* (DD-621), *USS Shubrick* (DD-639), *USS Gherardi* (D-637), *USS Rich* (DE-695), *USS Bates* (DE-68)

Frigates: *HMS Hotham* (K583), *HMS Tyler* (K576)

Corvettes: *Aconit*, *Renoncule*

Gunboats: *HNMS Soemba*, *Monitor Erebus* (I02)

Troop transport ships: *USS Bayfield* (APA-33), *HMS Empire Gauntlet* (F123), *USS Barnett* (APA-5), *USS Joseph T. Dickman* (APA-13)

The LCVP crew comprised four men: a coxswain, an engineer, a bowman and a sternman. This barge belonged to *LST 58*.
© USCG

LCVPs heading for the shoreline. *USS Augusta*, the Western Task Force's flagship, can be seen in the background. Admiral Kirk and General Bradley were both on board. © NARA

The German coastal artillery batteries entered into action as from 05:30. *USS Hawkins*, the target of a 155mm battery located in the Carentan sector, was forced into retreat. Six minutes later, the Allied warships received orders to open fire, 14 minutes ahead of the initial schedule. Simultaneously, the 203mm and 127mm gun turrets aboard the *Tuscaloosa* bombarded Tatihou Island. *USS Quincy* and *USS Glennon* engaged in combat against the batteries covering the north of Utah Beach. The battleships and heavy cruisers used observation planes to direct their fire, whereas the destroyers poised near the coast located their targets using binoculars and thanks to information provided by forward artillery observers on dry land.

The guns housed in *USS Nevada*'s turrets entered into action.
© NARA

The *Schrapnellmine* or *S-Mine 35* was a dreaded weapon. When it exploded, it set off from a height of around 90 centimetres and sent 360 small but deadly balls hurtling over a distance of twenty metres.
© Private collection

SECURING THE SAINT-MARCOUF ISLANDS

The American high command had decided to send a force to take control of the Saint-Marcouf Islands. Napoleon Bonaparte had had a military fort measuring 170 metres in diameter built on Île du Large. Following reports by aerial reconnaissance missions of traces of recent activity, the Allies feared that the enemy may have installed artillery pieces likely to bombard Force U. It was therefore decided that a small contingent be landed on the island to put a stop to any threat.

A detachment commanded by Lieutenant-Colonel Edward C. Dunn was formed by recruiting men from the 4th and 24th Cavalry Squadrons. At around 04:30, *Landing Ship Support 12* came to a halt a short distanced from the islands. Two dinghies were put to the water. Boarded by two 2-man crews, they set off in the dark of night. Corporal Harvey Olson and Private Thomas Killoran from the 4th Cavalry Squadron landed on Île de Terre. Sergeant John Zanders and Corporal Melvin Kenzie from the 24th Cavalry Squadron did likewise on Île du Large. These scouts armed with simple knives marked out the zone with their torches for the majority of the troop. An hour later, four Landing Craft Assault barges brought in 132 men. They encountered no opposition. Reconnaissance around the fort rapidly revealed that the island was devoid both of soldiers and of guns. Nineteen soldiers were nevertheless killed or wounded throughout the day by antipersonnel mines buried by the Germans and the odd shell fired on the islands.

A medical unit being transferred to a Landing Craft Medium. © NARA

BULL'S EYE FOR THE B-26 MARAUDERS

Armourers preparing bombs before loading them into the hold of a B-26 Marauder from the 387th Bombardment Group.
© USAAF

Naval bombardments were followed by aerial attacks. At 06:05, several B-26 Marauder medium bomber formations from the US 9th Army Air Force (323rd, 334th, 344th, 386th and 387th, 394th Bombardment Group) appeared to the north: the 323 planes were transporting sixteen 250-pound bombs. Equipped with instantaneous impact fuses, these weapons were designed to explode on impact.

Radio headset used by the crews of USAAF bombers.
© Private collection

The aim was to avoid creating craters likely to hinder the progression of vehicles on the beaches. Sixteen B-26s from the 397th Bombardment Group took part in the mission. As its nickname - *Brigdebusters* - suggests, the unit was specialised in the destruction of structural works. The planes were armed with 2,000-pound bombs capable of slashing open concrete bridges. The bombers flew at a maximum altitude of 5,000 feet under a cloud ceiling. In contrast with the heavy B-24 Liberator bombers that were to launch a perpendicular attack over the Omaha Beach sector, with the inefficiency we are all familiar with, the Marauders approached their target lengthways. Whilst 46 planes failed to release their cargo of bombs, the 293 others accomplished their mission (two B-26s and their crews were lost in a collision above England). A third of their weapons landed in the sea, the others exploding on the beach. Strings of bombs dropped by Major David Dewhurst Jr.'s 553rd Bomb Squadron hit the bull's eye, wreaking havoc in the German positions directly opposite the first wave of assault. The networks of barbed wire were blown to pieces and mines exploded prematurely.

The B-26 Marauder was used for high precision, low altitude attacks. Often, the enemy anti-aircraft defence had no time to react. © NARA

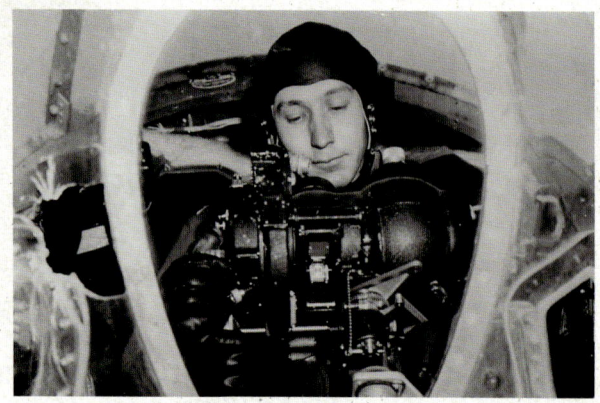

Once the target had been selected by the bomber, the Norden bombsight took over via automatic pilot and guided the plane during the final approach, correcting its coordinates if necessary. The sight then automatically activated the bomb drop when above the target. © NARA

Concurrently, 33 planes dropped 47 tonnes on the enemy batteries established in Maisy and Géfosse.

Their communication trenches were severed. Entrenched within their bunkers and shelters, the 75 men from the *919. GR's 3. Kompanie* huddled up along the walls, their hands hard over their ears as the explosions continued. Horrified, they anxiously awaited each impact, praying they would be spared. They shouted to evacuate their fear and to avoid suffering from serious ear damage at each blast. The impact was so violent that the blockhouses literally trembled on the spot. The P-47 Thunderbolt fighter-bombers finished the job with their rockets and machine guns. Several bunkers and ammunition holds were reduced to ruins. A young *Oberleutnant*,

'At first daylight the Isle St. Marcouf was observed on our starboard hand, while overhead aerial combat was observed between a German and allied airplane. The German plane was seen to go down north of the island. Enemy shell fire commenced shortly afterward with projectiles exploding in the water nearby. P.C. 1261., a control vessel off our port beam, took a direct hit and started to sink as we proceeded toward the beach [...]. While high and dry on the beach, two German ME109's strafed the beach immediately in front of us. Shrapnel struck the bow which superficially wounded one crewman. Both of these aircraft were downed before reaching the southern end of Utah Beach. Late in the evening we retracted from the beach toward deeper water, where we dropped the anchor and watched an elaborate display of anti-aircraft fire attempting to down a German intruder [...].'

Ensign Donald Eidemiller - LCT 594

Arthur Jahnke, aged just 23 at the time, was in command of *WN 5*. Entrenched inside an advanced observation post, he had escaped certain death.

Off shore, battleships and cruisers pursued their artillery duel with the German batteries. The destroyers positioned off Utah fired several hundred shells on their targets.

Without cover from the artificial smoke screen, *USS Corry* and *USS Fitch* became the targets of the German coastal batteries.

Leather jacket worn by the crews of USAAF bombers. © Private collection

The 'Lorraine' group was renamed No. 342 Squadron upon its arrival in Britain, where it specialised in bombardment missions by night, at medium or low altitude. © Rights reserved

THE MIST MAKERS

Twelve twin-engine Douglas Boston bombers from the 'Lorraine' No. 342 Squadron appeared off Utah. Their commander, Michel Fourquet, was a specialist in low altitude, high accuracy bombardments. The mission of these FAFL (Free French Air Forces) crews was to create a heavy smoke screen between the Saint-Marcouf islands and the Barfleur headland, in order to conceal the approach of the first landing barges. The holds contained huge two-metre cylinders equipped with exhaust pipes connected to bomb launcher controls.

The armed Bostons razed the horizon, just 15 metres above the water line and under the mantel of shells fired by the warships. Soon, dense white smoke formed a compact 10 kilometre-thick curtain. Mission accomplished! But on their return to England, two planes were reported missing. One had been damaged, the other - hit by the *Flak* - had crashed into the sea. *Sous-lieutenant* Canut, *Sergent* Pilote Boissieux and *Sergent* Henson all perished in the course of their mission.

H-HOUR

General Barton's 4th Infantry Division entered into action. At 06:30, 20 LCVPs transporting the 8th Infantry Regiment's 1st and 2nd Battalions (600 men) approached the Tare Green and Uncle Red sectors. The units were to take control of the beach exits and to join up with the airborne forces. For the occasion, the Regiment had been reinforced with the addition of a battalion from the 22nd Infantry Regiment. Eight LCTs, each transporting four Sherman DD tanks from the 70th Tank Battalion were to follow at ten-minute intervals.

From the very start, operations did not go according to plan. Three of the four ships in charge of guiding the barges towards their assault sectors fell

Helmet liner belonging to a seaman from *LCT 596*, found off Utah Beach. The ship transported the 70th Tank Battalion's B Company on the morning of the 6th of June. © A. Tournier collection

Medics tending to one of their compatriots. Although the beach was rapidly in Allied hands, the German artillery remained highly active. The men in the background have hollowed out foxholes. © NARA

victim to mines. The pilots and officers aboard the LCVPs tried in vain to distinguish characteristic features on the coastline before them, through the dense curtain of smoke and dust. Above them, P-47 Thunderbolt fighter bombers attacked enemy positions with rockets and machine guns. When they came within 400 metres of the shoreline, company commanders threw smoke bombs to inform the ships to increase their firing range. When the front of the barges grazed the sand and the ramps were lowered, the heavily laden assault troops thrust forward, trying to reach the dunes as quickly as possible. The dreaded deluge of enemy

USS CORRY'S LAST MISSION

The destroyer *USS Corry* (Gleaves-Class), brought into service in 1942, was assigned to water surveillance in the Pacific, the Mediterranean and the Atlantic. Its guns sunk the *U-801 U-Boot* on the 17th of March 1944. The following month it left Norfolk to head for Plymouth. On the 5th of June, the destroyer offered protection to a Force U convoy and took up position off Utah Beach. It fired several shells on its targets. However, the 210mm guns at the Crisbecq battery spotted *USS Corry* and *USS Fitch*, neither of which were concealed by the artificial smoke screen. The two ships initially managed to elude the bombs until, at 06:33, *USS Corry* hit a mine which immediately exploded under its keel, killing or wounding all the seamen in the neighbouring compartments. With its rudder blocked to the right and its engine room flooded, the *Corry*'s bow began to go under. As Lieutenant Commodore George Hoffman ordered for the crew to abandon ship, further salvoes of enemy gunfire hit the sinking ship. Several shells exploded amidst the shipwrecked seamen. Gunfire finally ceased at 08:30. The destroyers *USS Fitch* and *USS Hobson*, together with the *PT-99* launch then approached to rescue the survivors, many of whom were suffering from hypothermia after spending two hours in the Channel waters. Of the 19 officers and 265 seamen on board, 24 were killed and 60 wounded.

The servers of an Oerlikon gun, aboard *LCI(L) 322* firing on a target off Utah Beach. The gun's high angle suggests they are firing on a plane. Witness reports have since confirmed incursions by the *Luftwaffe*. © USCG

Men from a medical unit laden with stretchers landing on Utah Beach mid morning. © NARA

'Dawn has broken and, dimly in a haze of smoke, we can see the beach. Now it's our time. Men scramble to their feet. Equipment is adjusted. Lifebelts made more secure. For all around us, artillery shells are falling and, already, several boats have been hit. Rifles are loaded, with the safety taken off. The shore is now right off the bow. The coxswain signals me that we're about to touch down. The ramp is lowered, and the sergeant and I step off into four feet of water. I look behind me and men are already off the boat and scattered for protection against the bullets which are signing around us but, for the most part, hitting the water. It was a hell of a feeling. We had about five hundred yards of water to cross. We couldn't run 'cos the water was too deep. We couldn't crouch. We couldn't do anything except just what we did.'

Captain Alfred Birra
237th Engineer Combat Battalion
8th IR, 4th US Infantry Division.

gunfire failed to materialise. With the exception of the odd shell and a few salvoes from automatic rifles, the German defences were curiously silent. Barely 15 minutes later, the amphibious tanks put to the water 2,700 metres away could set to work.

Around 06:40, the Landing Craft Tanks (LCT) unloaded the 27 tanks from the 70th Tank Battalion, which immediately offered cover to the first waves of assault engaged in combat with the small garrison in control of *WN 5*. Four tanks were missing after their LCT hit a mine. Due to strong coastal currents, the first wave landed on the beach at Sainte-Marie-du-Mont - also summarily defended - two kilometres south of its planned zone.

The guns of the Azeville and Morsalines batteries were sufficiently out of range to pose no real threat to the beach. Those at the Saint-Marcouf battery retaliated in direction of the Allied ships. Scattered shells fired by German field artillery batteries exploded at regular intervals on the beach.

US Army gas mask.
© Private collection

Whereas *WN 5* had been put out of action by Allied bombs, other strongpoints were fit enough to retaliate. The German soldiers headed for their combat positions. © Private collection

Two companies from the 87th Chemical Mortar Battalion landed at 07:20 and formed a battery with their 120mm guns to deal with the targets identified by forward observers. Barely had it grounded when one Landing Craft Mechanized (LCM) suffered a bull's eye hit in the Green Beach sector. Unable to jump out of the barge, six sappers were killed. Losses were moderate compared to those on Omaha. At 07:30, less than 30 minutes after the Landings had begun, the men from the Ivy Division had successfully crossed the barbed wires and had reached the antitank wall that bordered the line of dunes around *WN 5*.

The 65th Armored Field Artillery Battalion and the 29th Field Artillery Battalion arrived around 09:30. Both sustained losses. LCT 458, which was transporting a 29th FAB battery, hit a magnetic mine. The explosion cost the lives of 39 artillerymen, wounding a further twenty.

The first waves of infantrymen wore assault jackets over their HBT M-1941 uniforms, coated with an anti-vesicant agent. © Private collection

These soldiers have thrown themselves to the ground to escape a large calibre shell. Low tide and the break of dawn indicate that the picture was taken early in the morning on the 6th of June. © NARA

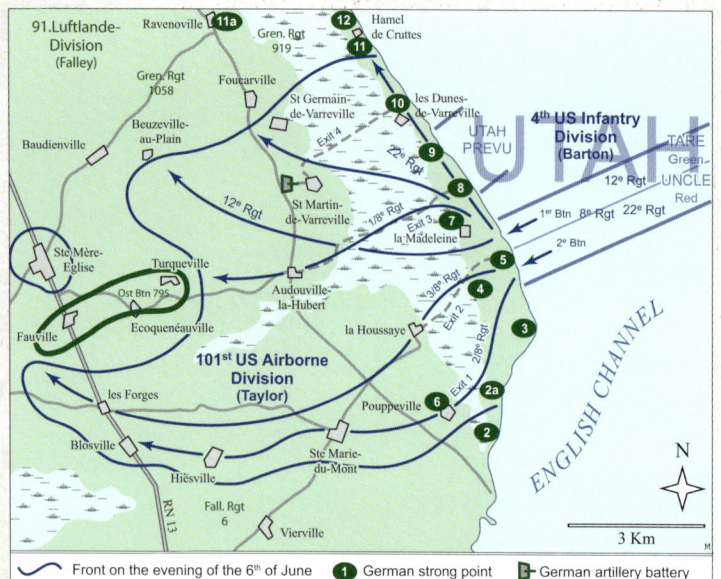

The Utah bridgehead on the evening of the 6th of June. © Y. Magdelaine

Theodore Roosevelt Jr., second in command of the division, arrived at the beach with his walking stick. At the age of 57, the Brigadier General was quick to realise that the men had not landed in the planned zone and took necessary measures. He told his men,

'We'll start the war from right here!'

He discussed the situation with Colonel James Van Fleet, commander of the 8th IR, and with Commodore James Arnold, in charge of clearing the beach for the US Navy.

Teams from Naval Combat Demolition Units (NCDU) removed the underwater obstacles in order to enable barges to safely ground, whilst teams of engineers from the 1st ESB cleared those on the beaches. The 237th Engineer Battalion was in charge of opening four 50 metre-wide passageways; however, given the timid German resistance, it was decided that the entire beach should be cleared. Sappers used TNT explosives to blow up the Czech hedgehogs, stakes and Belgian gates that blocked the beaches, whilst Companies A and C, helped by tankdozers, opened breaches in the antitank wall on the edge of the Red and Green sectors. They also blew up barbed wires using Bangalore torpedoes and they cleared the beach exits of mines. The entire zone was cleared within an hour.

US Navy RBZ receiver. During amphibious assaults, it enables seamen engaged in combat on land to receive instructions.
© Private collection

With tank support, the assault infantry was entrusted with reducing any defensive positions it came across. Discouraged by the prior bombardments, the soldiers in charge of defending Exits 1 and 2 (Sainte-Marie-du-Mont) were quick to give up their positions. At *WN 5*, Jahnke and his men were captured. They then boarded the destroyer that would take them to captivity. The enemy resistance nests were neutralised within two hours. The German positions located the furthest north were those who put up the staunchest resistance, preventing the American infantry from using Exit 3 (Audouville-la-Hubert).

The barges unloaded their incessant flow of men and vehicles. Beach Battalion teams built a command post from where they could organise

the arrival of future barges. The wounded were installed alongside the antitank wall pending their evacuation. By 10:00, the six battalions that comprised the 8th and 22nd RCT were hard at work. Guided by a forward observer, an artillery battery continued to fire on Exit 2, where a vast share of the traffic was to pass. Thankfully, the zone where the material and vehicles had been parked was not hit.

Fleet coordinated the attack on the last remaining strongpoints and launched an inland reconnaissance mission to locate the causeways. Columns of infantrymen and sappers, accompanied by tanks from the 70th Tank Battalion, then progressed inland. One tank was stopped in its tracks by a mine, whilst a second was destroyed by an antitank gun. Infantry companies crossed the flooded zone on foot. The 1/ and 2/22nd RCT spent seven hours wading their way through the marshes. With water up to their waists, the men struggled to progress, regularly tripping into underwater ditches. They had the added difficulty of having to avoid machine gunfire from the bunkers covering the north of the beach. They finally reached solid ground near Saint-Martin-de-Varreville, where they set up a temporary camp at Saint-Germain. The 3/22nd RCT in turn moved in a northwesterly direction to reduce the last enemy strongpoints and to protect the right flank of the bridgehead. The battalion passed the Dunes-de-Vareville and, at dusk, set up position to the south of Les Cruttes, near Exit 4.

Men and vehicles heading for the beach exits. The soldier in the foreground was not lucky enough to make it. A nurse has identified him by means of a medical card. © NARA

US Navy Corpsman satchel. © Private collection

TEDDY ROOSEVELT

Son to the former US President Theodore Roosevelt, Teddy Roosevelt had already distinguished himself during World War I. When the United States entered World War II in December 1941, he took a break from his career to serve his country, despite his age. Promoted to the rank of Brigadier General, 'Ted' Roosevelt was in command of the 1st USID 26th IR in North Africa. Always at the forefront, he was a highly appreciated officer. He was then sent to England as part of the Ivy Division's staff. Despite the reluctance of his superior, Major General Barton, who feared this may be a battle too far, Roosevelt nevertheless obtained permission to personally engage in the first wave of assault on Utah Beach. He died of a heart attack on the 12th of July in Méautis. He was buried with military honours in the temporary cemetery in Sainte-Mère-Église and was posthumously awarded the Medal of Honor. Later transferred to Colleville-sur-Mer, he now lies alongside his brother Quentin, killed in 1918.

Although often forgotten, signal units played a crucial role during combat. © NARA

A column from the 90th US Infantry Division taking a break. As indicated by the skull and crossbones on the road sign, mines were a permanent threat. © NARA

THE JUNCTION

In the afternoon, two 90th US Infantry Division battalions and glider units from the 82nd and 101st AB were in turn landed on Utah. The 2nd Battalion, 8th RCT advanced through Exit 1 towards Pouppeville. Near the locality, Captain George Mabry established contact with a para from the 101st AB. He also met General Taylor at 10:40, preceding General Gavin by just a few minutes. The junction was also made in Saint-Martin-de-Varreville.

The 3rd Battalion came across a tough German contingent armed with 88mm guns to the north of the village of Sainte-Marie-du-Mont. After short but intense combat, the Americans captured 100 German soldiers. Fifty were killed in the skirmish. An hour later, a tank entered Sainte-Marie. The other routes were secured in the afternoon, although Georgian soldiers from the

The General Purpose canvas musette bag could be used to carry extra ammunition.
© Private collection

THE RAFF FORCE

Colonel Edson Raff from the 507th PIR had been chosen by Ridgway to lead a small mechanised force that would land on Utah Beach. Although this appointment may have appeared to be a vexatious measure against an experienced parachute officer who demonstrated very little respect for his chief, the mission entrusted to the Raff Force remained vital: to join Sainte-Mère as quickly as possible. The force was composed of a company from the 325th GIR, 17 Sherman tanks from the 746th Tank Battalion and four M8 Greyhound Light Armoured Cars from the 4th Cavalry Squadron. The armoured column left Utah Beach at 14:00 to reach the Les Forges road junction without incident. However, it was then brought to a halt by a heavily armed enemy unit. Three tanks were destroyed, one after another. At a standstill, the Raff Force had no hope of receiving reinforcements. The men had no choice but to entrench themselves for the night.

795. Ost-Bataillon, positioned to the south of Turqueville, continued to resist, preventing the infantry from joining forces with the men from the 82nd AB. The 2/ and 3/8th RCT passed Les Forges to the south-west of Sainte-Marie-du-Mont. In Foucarville, combat continued well after nightfall. The Germans maintained pressure on the Americans from their positions in Beuzeville, but eventually decided to hoist the white flag shortly before midnight.

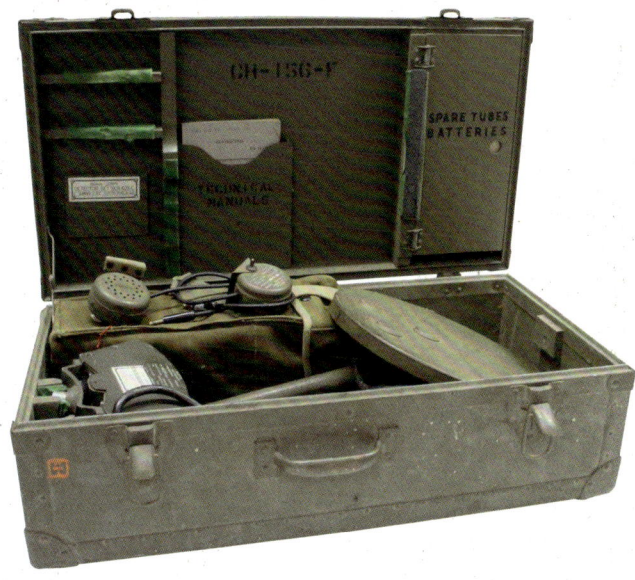

US Army SCR-625C mine detector. © NARA

Due to the congestion at the beach exits, infantry units advanced through the flooded zones. These men are still wearing their lifebelts, some of which have been inflated as a precaution. © NARA

This picture illustrates that danger could come from all around in the inland zones. © NARA

A TOLL A LONG TIME UNDERESTIMATED

Medical unit installed on the beach. After being sorted, the wounded were stabilised before being evacuated aboard hospital ships or direct to Britain. © NARA

Although still highly vulnerable, the bridgehead had nevertheless been established. The missions entrusted to the 4th Infantry Division met with equal success and with very few losses. Over several decades, when speaking of the losses sustained by the American troops on Utah Beach, the figure of 197 dead and 60 unaccounted for was put forward. The losses inflicted during the amphibious operation were low.

However, this figure must be put into context, for not all units present are included. The American historian Joseph Balkoski succeeded in establishing a far more accurate toll. The 4th Infantry Division lost a total of 311 men. The 90th USID's 359th Infantry Regiment sustained one death and one wounded soldier. Support units (artillery, engineer, reconnaissance, armoured) lost 278 men. Naval forces (US Navy, Royal Navy) and air forces (IX Bomber Command, IX Troop Carrier Command) respectively lost 235 and 185 men.

The airborne troops are also to be included in the overall toll. The 82nd and 101st Airborne Divisions in turn lost 1,259 and 1,240 men, which gives a new total of 3,510 losses. The 750 dead and 300 wounded during operation Tiger can then be added to this figure. The total is therefore comparable with his estimation of 4,700 men lost on Omaha. By the evening of D-Day, 20,000 men and 1,700 had been landed.

At a cost of bitter combat and substantial losses, the American parachutists had succeeded in provoking chaos amidst the enemy ranks, deprived of material and commitment. Their dispersal had proved salutary for it prevented the German command from grasping their intentions and from launching any large-scale counter-offensive.

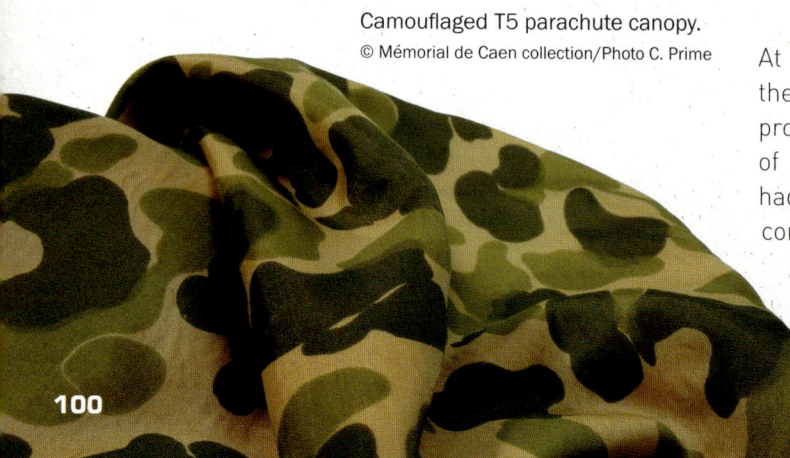

Camouflaged T5 parachute canopy.
© Mémorial de Caen collection/Photo C. Prime

Although the Utah bridgehead was solidly secured by the evening of the 6th of June, Ridgway and Taylor were not as yet crying victory. Half of their men were still scattered across the bocage landscapes and the Cotentin marshes. Small pockets of resistance continued to prevent certain units from joining forces.

Once the element of surprise had subsided, the enemy reorganised its troops, and reacted. Whilst the *LXXXIV Armeekorps* found itself in a perilous predicament, it was nevertheless aware of the American high command's intentions. On the 7th of June, soldiers from the *Ost Bataillon 439*, in position near Les Veys to the east of Carentan, had discovered a grounded barge in the Vire estuary. When they searched the vessel and the bodies of the soldiers on board, they discovered the VII Corps' battle plans. The next day, documents pertaining to the V Corps were found on the body of an American officer, fallen south of Vierville.

German prisoners digging graves under the watchful eye of a parachutist from the 101st AB. This picture appears to have been taken in Hiesville. Parachute suspending ropes have been used to mark out the graves. © NARA

Combined with reports from various units, this information enabled the Germans to ascertain that the VII Corps was to concentrate its efforts towards Valognes, and to take control of the port of Cherbourg and of Carentan, where they would join forces with units from the V Corps, landed on Omaha.

In Hiesville, the Catholic chaplain Francis L. Sampson blessing the parachutists killed in combat, the bodies of whom have been swathed in parachute canopies. 10th June 1944. © NARA

AFTER THE BATTLE

Glider pilots were a precious resource. Many of them were evacuated by Glider units. © NARA

Wounded in the arm, this para is being boarded onto an LCV by a team of Medics from the 1st ESB. © NARA

The 1st ESB installing makeshift headquarters alongside an antitank wall in the Uncle Red sector. © NARA

Over the days that followed the landings, shells continued to fall on the beach from time to time. These sailors from the 2nd Naval Beach Battalion have rushed inside their shelter just in time. © NARA

In a crater created by shellfire in the Madeleine dunes, the 4th Signal Company's transmitters in communication with a BC-654A radio supplied by a hand-powered generator. The Comanche Code Talker in the background is using a BC-611 walkie-talkie. © NARA

German prisoners, hands on heads, marching in procession towards the beach, pending their evacuation to Britain. © NARA

Among the German prisoners, the Americans were surprised to find Korean soldiers. Enlisted in the Japanese army, they had been captured by the Soviets during the Battle of Khalkhin Gol. Incorporated within the Red Army, they were requisitioned by the *Wehrmacht* to form *Osttruppen* battalions. © NARA

The US Navy and Royal Navy barges incessantly shuttled reinforcements in men and material. © USCG

PART 4

THE UTAH BRIDGEHEAD AFTER THE 6TH OF JUNE

THE SAINT-CÔME-DU-MONT BLOCKADE

The *FJR6* had received orders to defend the town of Carentan to the very last man, for its control prevented the American troops from establishing a junction with their bridgeheads. This small Norman town was at a strategic crossroads on the roads leading from Cherbourg to Bayeux and Saint-Lô. The fact that it was surrounded by marshes, with the Vire-Taute canal to the east and the Douve to the west, in no way facilitated the task facing the assailants. To add insult to injury, the Germans had flooded the river bed. The raised road towards Saint-Côme-du-Mont offered the only passable route. The *FJR6*'s *2. Bataillon* and *3. Bataillon*, together with a vast share of the *91. Luftlande Division*, *IR. 1058*, had managed to withdraw to Carentan and to prepare its defence. Marcks rapidly sent two *Osttruppen* battalions to the position, along with what remained of the *GR. 914* on its retreat from Isigny. Von der Heydte in turn placed his two battalions at the entrance to the road, facing northwards. Eastern volunteer troops were posted to the east, alongside the canal.

German parachutist's knee pads. © Vassas collection

Bradley ordered for the 101st AB, in position in the sector stretching from Chef-du-Pont to the mouth of the Douve, to take control of the locality in order to bridge the gap between Utah and Omaha. Despite having sustained heavy losses, the division had regained a relatively coherent organisation, which enabled Ridgway to efficiently plan the assault.

On the morning of the 7th of June, the 1/ and 2/506th PIR, the 2/501st PIR and the 3/327th GIR resumed their advance towards Saint-Côme. They bypassed the hamlet of Les Droueries and continued under enemy gunfire. At around 21:00, the 506th PIR's D Company reached the crossroads to the south of the village. The paras were as yet unaware that the house belonging to the Marie family, located at the junction, housed an *FJR6* command post and a medical unit. The Germans waited till the column had passed before opening fire. The paras hastily retreated, leaving five men behind.

Abandoned German material grouped together near the church in Saint-Côme. A keystone for the defence of the Carentan sector, the village was the theatre of bitter combat. © NARA

An M5 Stuart light tank from the 70th Tank Battalion was destroyed on the crossroads by a shot from a *Panzerfaust*. The body of the tank commander remained hanging from the gun turret for several days, hence the site's subsequent nickname of Dead Man's Corner.

Saint-Côme suffered a severe artillery bombardment. The Screaming Eagles resumed the attack to the south and the east; however, Von der Heytde's

Camouflaged M-38 helmet. This particular type of camouflage is often attributed exclusively to the *FJR6*, but not to the entire regiment. It was, however, also seen in use by other units. © Private collection

men, who were defending the crossroads, put up steadfast resistance for the entire day, launching several counter-offensives. Colonel Sink's men could finally enter Saint-Côme late afternoon. The *Fallschirmjäger* grouped together to the south of the locality. This unexpected retreat enabled the 501st PIR to cross the canal over the Douve without incident and to occupy the sector to the north-west of the Carentan-Périers road, in the commune of Méautis. Bridges were blown up and reconnaissance troops sent towards Isigny.

This *Fallschirmjäger* has covered his helmet with wiring to attach branches for camouflage. He also has an extra pocket on his sleeve, most likely to store a map.
© Rights reserved

Fabric pouch for gasmask specifically used by the *Fallschirmjäger*.
© Private collection

PURPLE HEART LANE

Rallied together to the south of Saint-Côme-du-Mont, the *Fallschirmjäger* managed to contain the American armoured detachments as the latter tried to break through the positions held by the Germans up to the 8th of June. Von der Heydte, who had established his command post in a farm belonging to the Ingouf family, ordered for his men to retreat. Joined by the survivors from the *III. GR. 1058*, the *II.* and *III. FJR6* crossed the canal over the Douve to establish a new line of defence to the north of Carentan, on either side of the road. Two *Ost-Bataillonen*, reinforced by elements from the *GR. 914*, had taken up position along the canal to the east of Isigny. Ridgway had no intention of affording the Germans the time to reorganise.

Inside of an M-38 helmet. The cut chin strap indicates that it has been taken from a lost soldier's body. © Private collection

The 502nd PIR was entrusted with the task of capturing the four bridges that controlled access to the north of Carentan and to Hill 30. The 327th GIR was in turn to set foot on the right bank of the Douve level with Brévands, as the 506th PIR attacked to the southwest. Two field artillery battalions were to provide support fire.

Shortly after midnight on the 10th of June, the 3/502nd PIR advanced along the road. The surrounding fields were flooded. They effortlessly crossed the first bridge, but as they approached the second, 88mm shells showered down on them, damaging the bridge deck. In the course of the afternoon, to enable the bridge to be crossed, a metallic beam was installed. A patrol,

M-1942 parachutist jacket used by the 101st AB.
© Private collection

A team of war correspondents immortalised the image of this Norman couple placing flowers on the body of one of their liberators in the Carentan sector. © NARA

sent on reconnaissance to inspect the rest of the route, reached the last bridge to find it blocked by a heavy Belgian gate. Spotted by the Germans, they retreated under intense gunfire coming from a farm and a hedge located just 400 metres from the road. An artillery barrage preceded Cole's counter-attack. To advance, the men crawled along the embankments. They crossed the third bridge one by one before being halted once more by mortar and machine gunfire. Two cruising Ju. 87 Stuka bombers attacked the American troops from low altitude. With 60 of its 80 men killed or wounded, I Company was no longer fit for combat. The 3/502nd PIR had reached the Carentan road but had lost over two thirds of its men in the process. This action earned the causeway the nickname of Purple Heart Lane. The paras then took cover in a field and awaited nightfall before attempting to cross the last bridge.

Cole was determined to neutralise the elements inside the Ingouf farm, a strategic defensive position for the Germans. At 06:15, a whistle blew. Under enemy gunfire, he led his men across the field and reached the abandoned farm. But the paras were quick to realise that the Germans were entrenched along the hedge just a few hundred metres away. In a hurry to be done with them, the officer ordered for his men to attach their bayonets to the barrels of their Garand rifles. Armed with a Colt 45 pistol, he launched a new charge which, this time, proved decisive.

The battalion had just broken through the first line of defence held by the *FJR6*, but at a cost of a heavy death toll. Cole now had 132 of an initial 250 men still fit for combat. He was later to be awarded the Medal of Honor by the U.S. Congress. He was killed in Holland a few months later. Von der Heydte withdrew his regiment after an ultimate counter-attack. One company was left to the rear to cover their retreat, under cover of smoke bombs.

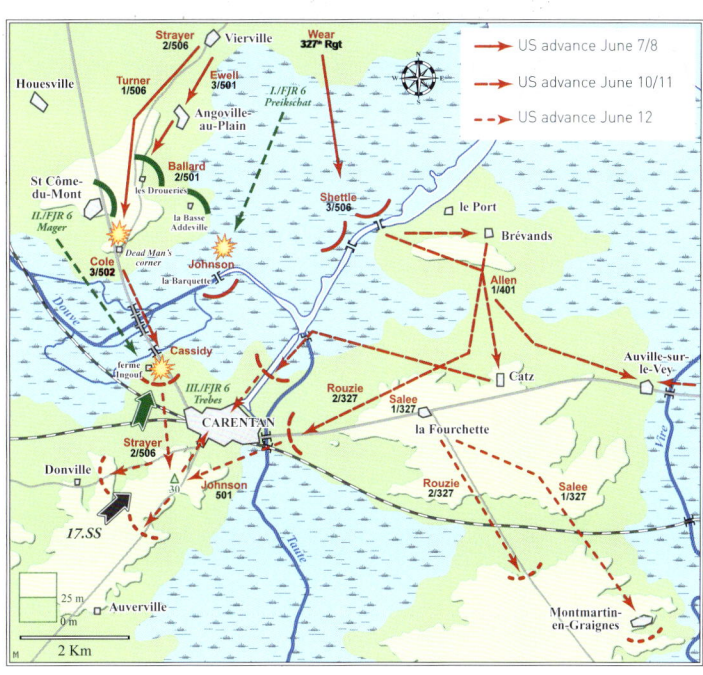

Battle of Carentan: 7th-12th June 1944. © Rights reserved

LP-42 flare pistol and Italian-made cartridge bag. The German troops made regular use of material recovered from other theatres of operation. © Private collection

THE BATTLE OF CARENTAN

Paras from the 101st AB in the streets of the freshly liberated town of Carentan. © NARA

Over the hours, the German units engaged in combat here and there. The 327th GIR crossed the Douve and secured Brévands and the surrounding area before dawn. The 3rd Battalion's A Company moved forwards towards Auville-sur-le-Vey and Catz. Glider units neutralised a heavily armed enemy detachment before reaching the two hamlets. At around 15:00, contact was established with the 29nd US Infantry Division reconnaissance group, commanded by Captain William H. Puntenney. The two American bridgeheads were now reunited.

Gravity knife used by the *Luftwaffe*. Each para was adequately equipped to cut his parachute suspending ropes. The knife was stored in a trouser pocket located at knee level. This one was found in Carentan. © Private collection

The glider units were to take control of access routes to Carentan, in particular the railway bridges and the road bridge on the way to Isigny. The men made quick progress before being stopped by enemy gunfire early evening, just 400 metres from the canal. Colonel Bud Harper, in command of the regiment in lieu of Colonel George Wear, who had been relieved from duty a few hours earlier, decided to continue the advance alongside the marina. Meanwhile, the men set down for the night. At around 10:00 the following morning, two companies crossed a small pedestrian footbridge over the Taute under gunfire from the first houses in Carentan. The gliders advanced several hundred metres under cover of the woods that ran alongside the dock, before being brought to a firm halt by machine gunfire from isolated men hiding in the same houses. To the west, the paras from the 506th PIR had reached the top of

With no jeep at their disposal, these 101st AB paras are using a *Kubelwagen* taken from *FJR6*. Exhausted Gliders can be seen seated in front of Désiré Ingouf's café-restaurant at the Houlgate junction on the RN13 trunk road. © NARA

A Stug III, destroyed during a counter-attack by the *Gotz von Berlinchingen*. © NARA

Three paras proudly posing in front of the war memorial in Carentan. © NARA

Hill 30 near La Billonnerie, where they found the 501st PIR, creating a loop around the town.

Naval artillery bombarded the site the following night, in order to veil the troop movements in preparation for a new assault. On the morning of the 12th, the American attack proved pointless. Von der Heydte had taken the initiative of evacuating the town in order to save his regiment from destruction. At 06:00, the 2/506th PIR attacked to the south and finally occupied Hill 30, whilst the 1/401st GIR headed for the town centre, which it reached at 07:30. The two other 101st AB regiments moved in a south-westerly direction before being halted by the first elements from the *Götz von Berlichingen*, who had arrived the previous evening.

The Allied capture of Carentan was a huge blow to the *7. Armee. Generalleutnant de Waffen-SS* Ostendorff, commander of the *Götz* division, was furious and immediately lashed out at Von der Heydte, accusing him of having abandoned the town without orders to do so. He had him arrested until his trial under court martial; however, the parachute officer was spared the worst outcome thanks to his superior, Meindl's intervention.

With support from *Götz* division assault guns, the *FJR6* counter-attacked to the northeast of the town on the night of the 12th to the 13th of June, whilst the 506th and 501st PIRs attacked the southwest. The *Fallschirmjäger* overpowered the American paras and advanced within reach of the railway station. Although Lieutenant-Colonel Strayer managed to stabilise the situation, it was at a cost of heavy losses. At around 16:30, the arrival of the 2nd Armored Division's Combat Command A, together with elements from the 29th US Infantry Division, forced the enemy into retreat towards the heights to the south of the town. Units from the three 101st AB regiments engaged in the operation managed to take hold of the Manoir de Donville after fierce close-range combat. The Battle of Bloody Gulch brought the Battle of Carentan to a close.

FJR6 Sanitätstornister sanitary backpack. © Rights reserved

THE GRAIGNES MASSACRE

Since the 6th of June, groups of parachutists from the 501st and the 507th PIR had been entrenched in the village of Graignes with their commander, Major Arthur Johnson. A medical post had been established in the church and the command post in the village school. Look-outs kept watch from the belfry. The locals provided the troops with food.

Patrols were sent to inspect the surrounding area. Skirmishes became increasingly frequent over the days. On the 10th of June a motorcycle patrol and a truck were intercepted near Saint-Georges-de-Bohon. By the Sunday morning, the village was totally surrounded. Grenadiers from the *Waffen-SS Gotz von Berlichingen* division attacked during Sunday mass. The combat that ensued was particularly violent. The last German attack finally totally overwhelmed the American positions. The paras withdrew in a disorderly fashion across the marshes under cover of the night, leaving their wounded buddies behind. Three seriously injured soldiers were taken to the church sanctuary. Fourteen paras, Fathers Leblastier and Lebarbanchon, and two women, were executed. The village was then pillaged before being burned.

WHO HOLDS MONTEBOURG, HOLDS CHERBOURG

Three destroyed US Army vehicles placed at the entrance to Montebourg as a warning. © NARA

American assault jacket used by the 4th US Infantry Division. Unpopular among the soldiers, some nevertheless used it, after cutting out the lower part.
© Private collection

In order to create a blockade preventing any access to the peninsula, Von Schlieben had established a line of defence south of Montebourg. From the heights, the Germans benefited from an excellent look-out point over the entire sector. The principal line of defence (*Hauptkampflinie*) relied on the artillery batteries in Crisbecq, Azeville and Quinéville. Reinforcements had been sent into the area. Elements from the *Sturm Battalion AOK7 243. ID*, who had rushed down from Cherbourg by bicycle, came to offer support to *Oberleutnant* Günther Keil, in charge of defending the sector. A *Kampfgruppe* from the *77. ID* was also on its way. The zone was covered by five artillery batteries, Nebelwerfers (multiple rocket launchers) and 88mm guns. The guns at the Morsalines and Videcosville batteries had been removed from their casemates to be installed in advanced positions. Heavy machine guns and mortars, located behind the Coisel stream covered the southern front.

The US troops set off on the morning of the 8th of June. The 8th Infantry Regiment advanced between the rubble along the Valognes-Carentan railway line and the RN13 trunk road. The paras from the 505th PIR took control of Neuville-au-Plain in the course of the afternoon. Three battalions endured a violent attack to their right as they approached the village of Écausseville and its huge 150 metre-long airship hangar. The sector was defended by elements from the *922. GR* and the *Sturm-Bataillon AOK. 7*. Astutely concealed mortars, 88mm guns and machine guns thwarted the American attacks. Heavy losses were sustained on both sides. E Company lost sixty men. The hangar was finally reached, and the Germans decided to abandon Écausseville under cover of the night. No more fortunate, the 12th Infantry Regiment lost 300 men before Emondeville. The 505th PIR had managed to progress as far as Grainville, which they found deserted.

The assault was relaunched on the 9th of June. The 82nd AB received orders to take control of a hill located between the station in Montebourg and Le Ham. With support from tactical aviation and artillery, the 1/505th PIR reached the station, obliging the Germans to retreat towards Le Ham. In contrast, the 2/325th GIR was at a standstill and remained so until dusk. The following morning, trooper and glider elements crossed the railway track and advanced, their rifles fitted with bayonets, amidst the marshes, covered by a thick artificial smoke screen. However, the Germans continued to fire at random, inflicting severe losses among their adversaries, who were advancing without the slightest cover. Yet the All Americans' tenacity finally paid off and they reached the outskirts of the town. After one last assault launched early evening,

Alter Art cap worn by a non-commissioned infantry officer from the *Heer*. © Vassas collection

they entered the devastated locality, now devoid of any German occupants.

The 12th Infantry Regiment was struggling before Montebourg, the keystone of the German defensive system in the sector and, consequently, bitterly defended by soldiers from the *GR. 1058* and *729*. A German counter-attack launched on the 10th was driven back by the naval artillery. Following repeated bombardments, the town was no more than a pile of smoking rubble. On the 12th of June, the front line was stable from the north of the Merderet to Montebourg.

Thanks to unit progression on either side of the town, Barton could launch a new assault on the 19th of June, taking the defensive line held by the Keil *Kampfgruppe* from the rear. The combat group had no choice but to retreat. The Americans entered Montebourg at dawn on the 20th of June. The road to Cherbourg was now open.

The airship hangar in Écausseville was, all in all, spared by the combat. It was used by the US Army for storage and repairs. © Rights reserved

This German soldier has been literally buried in his trench by the American artillery. © NARA

QUINÉVILLE

WN 106 was a major fortified strongpoint built by the Germans in Quinéville, to the north of Utah Beach. *Oberst* Triepel, commander of the *1261. HKAA* had established his command post there. A battery armed with four 105mm K331 howitzers was positioned on Mont Coquerel.

Task Force Barber was in charge of neutralising this resistance nest. The 22nd Infantry Regiment's progression was hindered by elements from the *922. GR*. Fontenay-sur-Mer fell into American hands on the 12th of June. The garrison occupying Ozeville entrenched itself inside an artillery position. After short yet intense combat, it finally hoisted the white flag. 1st Lieutenant Dewhurst from I Company climbed onto the roof of a bunker, in order have the firing ceased. Suddenly, he collapsed, hit by a German gun. His enraged fellow soldiers rushed forth, killing a vast share of the garrison. Two days later, the three 22nd Infantry Regiment battalions attacked Quinéville from the west, whilst the 9th Infantry Division's 3/39th IR attacked from the south. The Germans continued to resist until late evening.

On the 12th of June, an officer or an interpreter from the 4th US Infantry Division talking to an *Oberleutnant* from the *Heer*, the latter seeming willing to cooperate. © NARA

These paras from the 502nd and 508th PIRs were mistakenly dropped in the immediate vicinity of Saint-Marcouf, in the early hours of the 6th of June, before the Germans returned there. The village was only completely liberated on the 8th of June. © NARA

AZEVILLE AND CRISBECQ

Concurrently, the 22nd Infantry Regiment advanced along the coastal sector, sustaining losses caused by enemy strongpoints and artillery fire. After wading for long hours through the marshes, the US infantry reached the heights in the vicinity of the Azeville and Crisbecq batteries, located 1,500 metres from each other. It was the regiment's mission to take control of both. These fortified positions comprised concrete casemates, shelters and depots, linked together via a huge network of underground galleries. Machine guns, antitank guns, barbed wires and minefields offered protection around the site perimeter. Mistakenly dropped in the sector, the paras from the 502nd PIR had already tried to capture the sites in vain.

The Americans launched the attack on the 7th of June. As it approached Crisbecq, the 1st Battalion was subjected to a counter-attack from antitank guns. The assailants were taken by surprise by a flanking attack, before making a chaotic retreat. The scene repeated itself before nearby Azeville. Two battalions were driven back by the violently defiant *Sturm Abteilung AOK 7*. Once more, intervention from the naval artillery enabled the Allies to stabilise their positions. Early afternoon on the following day, the 1st Battalion resumed its attack on Crisbecq, with support from M10 Tank Destroyers. After intense naval bombing, the GIs penetrated the position and engaged in combat with the defenders entrenched inside the concrete bunkers. *Oberleutnant* Zur see Walter Ohmsen contacted *Hauptmann* Trieber in Azeville and asked him to open fire on the partly captured battery. Salvoes of shellfire showered down on the American infantrymen as they hastily withdrew from a German counter-attack: 98 US soldiers were captured. The attack launched on the morning against the Azeville battery had been no more successful. A 356mm shell fired by the battleship *USS Nevada* shot straight through one casemate, from one side to the other, without blowing up, but killing all the gunners inside.

A 4th US Infantry Division machine gun section on the move in the sector around the Marmion farm in Ravenoville. © NARA

Oberleutnant zur See Ohmsen was indoctrinated by German propaganda. A total of 307 German soldiers were killed as they tried to defend the Crisbecq battery. Almost as many Americans died to capture the position.
© Rights reserved

Since the sieges on Crisbecq and Azeville were costing General Barton and his men precious time, he decided to bypass them. The following day, the 22nd Infantry Regiment's 3rd Battalion entered the perimeter of the Azeville battery, with tank cover. Although several armoured vehicles were damaged by mines, the infantry nevertheless took possession of the first bunkers and, at around 12 noon, they reached the casemates inside which the garrison had taken refuge. The only surviving tank fired on the fortifications whilst an assault team tried, unsuccessfully, to blow up the armoured doors with explosives. Armed with a flamethrower, Private Riley aimed the fire jet towards the steel door. The heat finally detonated the ammunition. Convinced that any resistance would be in vain, *Leutnant* Kattnig surrendered with his 168 men.

A few hundred metres away, Omhsen received orders to cease firing and to retreat without delay. The last gun was destroyed. On the night of the 11th to the 12th of June, the *Leutnant* and his 78 fellow escapees furtively meandered their way through the American lines and headed for the marshes. They joined forces with the other German lines in Aumeville at around 03:00. Early in the morning, the Americans entered the battery to discover some seriously wounded Germans, together with around a hundred American soldiers, captured over the previous days. For his feats of arms, Omhsen was awarded the *Ritterkreuz des Eisernes Kreuzes* (Knight's Cross of the Iron Cross) on the 14th of June.

US Army infantry non-commissioned officer's individual equipment. © Private collection

Bag for storing demolition charges.
© Private collection

UTAH, THE LOGISTICS BASE

As soon as the battle was over, the units in charge of logistics took possession of the beach. Whereas the American command had planned to build an artificial harbour at Omaha Beach to bring in supplies to the US V Corps, it contented itself with installing an artificial dock off Utah, since Cherbourg was to rapidly take over. This beach installation was supposed to be in operation for just four weeks.

From the 7th to the 9th of June, nine old and decommissioned cargos and warships were deliberately scuttled 900 metres off the shoreline to enable medium tonnage cargoes to anchor, so that barges and DUKW amphibious trucks could unload in a sheltered environment.

The US Navy was obliged to constantly adapt the blockship installation plan. During its installation, *SS Benjamin Contee* became a target and was shelled by German guns. *SS David O. Saylor* was

Composition of Gooseberry G-1 (Utah Beach, Sainte Marie-du-Mont)

Blockships: *SS George S. Wasson* (N° 575), *SS Matt W. Ransom* (N° 560), *SS Benjamin Contee* (N° 558), *SS David O. Saylor*, *SS Vitruvius*, *SS Victory Sword* (N° 368), *MS West Honaker* (N° 361), *MS West Cheswald* (N° 364), *SS West Nohno* (N° 353), *SS Willis A. Slater*, *SS Sahale*.

From their command post, these seamen were in constant contact with the barges as they approached the beaches. They communicated by means of an optical Morse code projector and a megaphone. © NARA

Gooseberry G1 Blockships. © NARA

forced to withdraw to escape similar shellfire but was finally in a position to be scuttled on the afternoon of the 8th of June. *SS Vitrivius* met with the same fate. Unaccustomed to being fired upon, the civilian crews on the tugs refused to put themselves in a dangerous situation.

At 08:30 on the 8th of June, the stern of the destroyer *USS Glennon* was blown away by a mine. The minesweepers *USS Staff* and *USS Threat* came to the rescue. At 09:20, it was the destroyer *USS Rich*'s turn to hit a mine. Damage was minimal; however, the ship was later shaken by successive explosions at intervals of just a few minutes. This concentration of vessels became a priority target for the German guns. Fire broke out aboard *USS Rich* and the ship sank in less than 15 minutes: 91 seamen were killed and 64 unaccounted for, from a total crew of 213 men.

USS Glennon's rear was anchored to the seabed and the ship could not be towed. Most of its crew

US Navy waterproof parka. © Private collection

123

The Gooseberry installed on Utah Beach supplied the US VII Corps up to late August 1944. © NARA

members were transhipped to *USS Staff*. The men still on board did their best to lighten the ship's rear. Fuel was pumped to the front, deep loads and part of the material on board were thrown overboard. The crew returned to try to save the ship the following day, but their mission was to prove vain. A German battery installed near Quinéville opened fire on the immobile vessel. Although the first salvo missed its target, the others were more accurate, despite counter-attacks fired from the Allied fleet. Two shells were to seal the fate of *USS Glennon*. Commodore Johnson ordered for the ship to be abandoned: 25 men were killed and 38 wounded.

Operations were also hindered by incessant *Luftwaffe* bombardments by night and by the omnipresence of mines. At around midday on the 8th of June, HMS Minster was destroyed by a mine, four kilometres from the Saint-Marcouf islands. All 58 crew members, at the mess at the time, were killed. Two days later, other bombs fell in the vicinity of *SS Victory Sword* and *MS West Cheswald*, without causing damage. *SS Honaker* was hit by two projectiles the same day. The blockship crews in turn shot down several aircraft before abandoning ship around the 15th of June.

The coastal currents did nothing to help Allied operations, many ships drifting off course. One example, *SS Matt W. Ransom*, drifted 300 metres before the explosives loaded into its double-base hull blew up. Thankfully, the tugs managed to reposition the vessel in its planned alignment before it filled with water. Finally, the original straight line had been transformed into two, slightly curved lines. However, independently of these mishaps, the Gooseberry G1 proved to be perfectly suited to the slope of the beach and the currents at rising tide. It was reinforced with the addition of two further blockships after the storm that began on the 19th of June 1944.

SS CHARLES MORGAN

Contrary to common belief, the *Luftwaffe* was particularly active during the first weeks that followed the D-Day Landings, the destruction of *SS Charles Morgan* at 04:00 on the 10th of June offering but one illustration. Built in 1943, this Liberty Ship was hit by a 250kg airdropped bomb. The port side deck and hull were torn open. The ship sank in the shallow waters, its bow remaining above sea level. The US Navy tried to refloat the ship before finally giving up and declaring it as lost. One crew member and seven soldiers lost their lives in the shipwreck.

US Navy troops setting up their bivouac for the night. © NARA

AND THE BEACH BECAME A HARBOUR

As from the very first days, Utah Beach was intended to support a daily traffic of 2,500 tonnes of freight. Finally, a daily load in the region of 5,000 tonnes arrived on the beach.

The barges grounded direct on the sand to unload men, vehicles and material. They then had to wait for high tide to head back to the high seas. DUKW trucks and Rhino ferries - low draught barges equipped with powerful outboard engines - were used to unload the ships anchored one or two kilometres from the shoreline.

On the 13th of June, floating metallic structures referred to as bombardons were moored off shore to serve as breakwaters. As from the 16th of June, the Seabees from the 25th Naval Construction Regiment (NCR) linked the 25 pontoons together to form three 500 metre-long floating docks. These docks were linked with the shore via floating causeways. Low-tonnage barges such as LCVPs

LCT 525 from Flotilla 4 mooring on a floating pontoon linked with Utah Beach via a causeway. © NARA

A Sherman M4A2 Ile de France tank from the *12e Régiment de Chasseur's d'Afrique* leaving *LCT 517* to land in France. On the front glacis plate, its crew has welded the plaque of the Somua S35 tank it used when serving in Africa. © NARA

Female auxiliaries landed on Utah Beach on the 14th of July. © NARA

and Rhino ferries could accost by the pontoons to unload their cargoes, which were immediately transported towards the storage zones located 4 kilometres from the beach by endless columns of trucks. A railway line was even built to increase the pace of deliveries. Military camps with tents were installed across hundreds of hectares.

Utah had become a hive of activity. The men from the US Navy controlled ship movements and logistic operations. They also repaired any damaged vessels. However, the vast share of port manoeuvres was ensured by Major General Caffey's 1st ESB. Initially comprised of 19,500 men, the brigade's numbers increased to around 70,000 over

The Seabees from the 111th Naval Construction Battalion attending a religious service on the 18th of June 1944. The sky is still clear. The same did not apply the following day. © NARA

the weeks to follow. The brigade finally left Cotentin in December 1944. It contributed towards the restoration of the port of Le Havre before heading for the Pacific to take part in the assault on Okinawa in April 1945.

Gooseberry G1 was sorely hit by the storm that raged across the English Channel from the 19th to the 22nd of June 1944. The peninsula generally protects the east coast against westerly winds, but not against those blowing from the northeast. The breakwaters and causeways were in a poor state and 212 barges had grounded. The Rhino ferries had been given a particularly rough ride. A total of 1,669 tonnes of material were nevertheless unloaded from the 20th to the 22nd of June.

From June to November 1944, Gooseberry G1 processed some 725,000 tonnes of material, 220,000 vehicles and 836,000 men. A total of 40,000 wounded soldiers and 60,000 German prisoners were also evacuated via the beach.

Some 10,000 Seabees from the 25th Naval Construction Regiment (NCR) were engaged on Utah and Omaha. Their main mission was to manoeuvre the Rhino ferries and to conduct maintenance on the pontoons and floating causeways. ©USCG

MINES, A PERMANENT THREAT

All inland areas were densely mined, with virtually all types of mine. Antitank mines and S-mines ('Bouncing Betties') were found in large numbers... Generally speaking, mines were scattered all over to such an extent that all fields were suspected to be infested and were consequently systematically inspected before being crossed. Approximately 4,500 tonnes of bombs were removed during operations on the beach and in flooded zones.

BIBLIOGRAPHY

Ambrose (Stephen E.), *D Day: June 6, 1944: The Climactic Battle of World War II*, Simon & Schuster, 1995.

Badsey (Stephen), *Utah Beach, Battle Zone Normandy*, Sutton Publishing, 2004.

Balkoski (Joseph), *Utah Beach, 6 juin 1944*, Histoire & Collections, 2015.

Department of the Army Historical Division, *Utah Beach à Cherbourg*, Foxmaster and Pozit Press, 1994.

Gawne (Jonathan), *Spearheading D-Day - American Special Units in Normandy*, Histoire & Collections, 1998.

Laurenceau (Marc), *D-Day, Hour by Hour*, OREP éditions, 2018.

McManus (John C.), *The Americans at D-Day: The American Experience at the Normandy Invasion*, Forge Books, 2005.

Prime (Christophe), *La Bataille du Cotentin, 6 juin – 15 août 1944*, Tallandier, 2019.

Quellien (Jean), *Normandy 44*, OREP éditions, 2015.

Shiletto (Carl), *Utah Beach-Ste Mere*, Pen and Sword, 2001.

Zaloga (Steven J.) et Gerrard (Howard), *Le Jour J : Utah Beach les parachutages américains*, Osprey Publishing, 2012.

ACKNOWLEDGEMENTS

The author and Editions OREP would like to thank all the collectors who were kind enough to contribute towards the compilation of this book, in particular Pascal Hourblin, Patrick Vassas, Adrien Tournier, David Brunet and all the others, who know who they are.

I would also like to pay tribute to the work by the museums that relate these events: the Utah Beach D-Day Museum in Sainte-Marie-du-Mont, the Airborne Museum in Sainte-Mère-Église and the D-Day Experience in Saint-Côme-du-Mont.

OREP EDITIONS

Zone Tertiaire de NONANT - 14400 BAYEUX
Tel.: (33) 02 31 51 81 31 - **Fax:** 02 31 51 81 32
E-mail: info@orepeditions.com - **Website:** www.orepeditions.com
Editor: Grégory Pique - **Editorial coordination:** Joëlle Meudic - **English translation:** Heather Inglis
Graphic design - Layout: Antoine Salmon - **OREP éditions**

Cover credits: Men from a medical unit laden with stretchers landing on Utah Beach mid morning. © NARA ; T5 parachute harness belonging to the 501st PIR. © Private collection
ISBN: 978-2-8151-0463-0 - Copyright OREP 2019 - Legal deposit: 3rd quarter 2019